THE END OF LIFE

contributors

GEORGE WALD
U.S. VON EULER
NATHAN A. SCOTT, JR.
ALEXANDER COMFORT
KRISTER STENDAHL

The End of Life

A DISCUSSION AT THE NOBEL CONFERENCE

organized by *Gustavus Adolphus College, St. Peter, Minnesota, 1972*

edited by

JOHN D. ROSLANSKY

Woods Hole, Massachusetts

1973
NORTH-HOLLAND PUBLISHING COMPANY
AMSTERDAM · LONDON
FLEET ACADEMIC EDITIONS, INC. − NEW YORK

1973 © NORTH-HOLLAND PUBLISHING COMPANY — AMSTERDAM

Library of Congress Catalog Card Number: 73-77077
ISBN North-Holland: 0 7204 6035 2
ISBN American Elsevier: 0 444 10524 7

Publishers:
NORTH-HOLLAND PUBLISHING COMPANY — AMSTERDAM
NORTH-HOLLAND PUBLISHING COMPANY, LTD. — LONDON

Sole distributors for the U.S.A. and Canada:
Fleet Academic Editions, Inc.
156 Fifth Avenue, New York, N.Y. 10010

Printed in The Netherlands

Editor's Acknowledgement

The End of Life discussions of the 1972 Nobel Conference are reproduced in this, the eighth volume of the series. Representatives from universities, colleges, and high schools were among the thousands who convened to participate in a serious effort to probe rationally one of the greatest predicaments of mankind.

As in previous years gratitude is due to the Arnold Ryden Foundation, the Tozer Foundation, the Bremer Foundation and the Board of Education and Church Vocations of the Lutheran Church in America for their continued support of the Nobel Conference which originally was initiated by the contribution of the Hill Family Foundation.

The Nobel Foundation supplied a photograph to accompany the Tribute to Arne Tiselius by Professor U.S. von Euler. All of these contributions were significant to the development and success of the Nobel Conference series.

John D. ROSLANSKY

Contents

Tribute to Arne Tiselius 1902—1971

This eighth volume of the Nobel Conference Lectures at Gustavus Adolphus College honors the memory of Arne Kaurin Tiselius, winner of the 1948 Nobel Prize in Chemistry.

Arne Tiselius had close connections with the Gustavus Adolphus College. In May 1963, when the College dedicated the Nobel Hall of Science, he received with 25 other Nobel Laureates an Honorary Degree from the College and addressed the Convocation. He whole-heartedly endorsed Dr. Seaborg's suggestion to continue and develop the association between Gustavus Adolphus College and the Nobel Laureates, which materialized in the much appreciated annual Nobel Conferences.

Born in Stockholm in 1902, Tiselius started his scientific career at the early age of 24 in Uppsala, when he became interested in protein chemistry. In 1930 he published his thesis on "The moving boundary method of studying the electrophoresis of proteins" which opened up new avenues for protein research of greatest consequences for chemistry and biology. Clinical chemistry received a new impetus by the separation and identification of the different serum protein fractions called alpha-, beta-, and gamma-globulins. The importance of the gamma-globulins for the immunological defence of the body is today generally recognized and appreciated. His work in this area has fomented research all over the world.

His interests became later directed to chromatography, and his classification of the different principles in this type of separation of chemical entities soon became generally accepted. In 1948 he received the Nobel Prize in Chemistry in recognition of "his research on electrophoresis and adsorption analysis, especially for his discoveries concerning the complex nature of the serum proteins".

Tiselius held many important positions in the academic and scientific world. He was for many years member and later chairman of the Nobel Committee for Chemistry and served also as member, vice-president, and president of the Nobel Foundation. As president of the International Chemistry Union he found many opportunities to promote friendship and scientific collaboration among his colleagues.

Tiselius himself pursued and encouraged others to pursue important research in a variety of fields. His personal qualities and quiet authority created an atmosphere and a scientific climate which made research flourish. He had a deep feeling for international cooperation on a wider scale, as evidenced lately by his keen interest in the Nobel Symposium dealing with "The place of value in a world of facts". At the time of his death he was engaged in a world-wide project aiming at coordinating the scientific potentials as well as the good will of a number of high-ranking scientific institutions in different areas across national boundaries. It is to be hoped that his intentions will be carried to success in the same humanitarian and warm-hearted spirit as characterized its originator.

U.S. von EULER
Royal Caroline Institute, Stockholm

George WALD

Origin of death*

DR. GEORGE WALD is one of the best known teachers in America. In 1966 he was one of the "ten outstanding teachers in America" pictured on the cover of TIME magazine. In 1967 he won the Nobel Prize for his basic research in regard to the presence of vitamin A in the retina.

What earned him his greatest adulation from students throughout America was his speech at M.I.T. on March 4, 1969, entitled "A Generation in Search of a Future".

The speech, which touched on the major problems facing students growing up in this generation, was published in full by the Boston Globe and subsequently by several other major newspapers. The Boston Globe distributed 87,000 reprints of the speech. A tape of the speech was made available for broadcast and it was also transcribed on a long play record. It is estimated that the total number of people who have heard or read the speech runs into the millions.

Dr. Wald was born in New York City and received his education at New York University and Columbia University (Ph.D. 1932). He arrived at Harvard in the fall of 1934 as a tutor in the biochemical sciences and has been a fixture there since. He now holds the title of Higgins Professor of Biology.

When one has wondered over the years about the origin of life, as I have done, one comes inevitably to ask oneself, just what kind of thing is one trying to bring forth? Need those first primitive organisms on the earth, for example, have had such complex apparatuses of reproduction as all organisms possess today? And then one comes to the curious question: Need those first organisms have died? Because if they didn't need to die, they needn't at least be in such a hurry to reproduce. And this brings one to this question of the origin of death.

For not all living creatures die. An amoeba, for example, need never die; it need not even, like certain generals, fade away. It just divides and becomes two new amoebas.

In fact, death seems to have been a rather late invention in evolution. One can go a long way in evolution before encountering an authentic corpse. This is the journey that I would like to make with you. What I should like to do, of course, is to begin with the first living organism on this planet and then pursue evolution onward, asking the question: When did the first organism appear that cultivated the habit of dying? But that is just what I can't do. As in so many other evolution stories, I have to be content with a poorer thing, and that is to discuss this transition in terms of contemporary organisms, of organisms alive today.

Let us begin with a familiar, single-celled organism, the amoeba. Its nucleus divides by pinching into two equal halves, then the whole amoeba divides. Thus we have two organisms where we started with one. This is the usual way single-celled organisms, plant and animal, tend to reproduce, just by simple division: so-called fission.

Occasionally they do something a little different. Reproduction in the single-celled organism *Paramecium* is usually by fission, but sometimes it engages in what we call *conjugation*. Two organisms, each containing a large nucleus (macronucleus) and a small nucleus (micronucleus), come together side-to-side. Then the cuticle breaks down between them. The macronucleus is by and large the working nucleus. The micronucleus represents a store of genetic material. The next thing that happens is that the macronuclei disintegrate and the micronuclei divide. Then something very interesting happens that makes one think a little of sexual reproduction; there is an exchange of micronuclei, of genetic material. Then the *Paramecia* separate, the micronuclei divide repeatedly, then the *Paramecium* divides repeatedly. One ends up with eight brand new *Paramecia* just like the pair with which we started.

In the generation just before mine there was a very distinguished zoologist named Loren Woodruff. He began to publish a series of papers, the first of which was entitled something like "Two hundred generations of *Paramecium aurelia* without conjugation". We waited a few years and another paper came out with a title something like "Five hundred generations of *Paramecium aurelia* without conjugation". Finally this series reached its culmination in a paper entitled "Eleven thousand generations of *Paramecium aurelia* without conjugation". So Professor Woodruff lived a happy and useful life, and convinced all of us that *Paramecium* can live indefinitely without conjugation.

But in the course of these researches Woodruff made another discovery. You see, every morning he'd come into his laboratory and find two *Paramecia* where he'd left one the night before; so he'd carefully separate them. One *Paramecium*, he thought, can't conjugate. But that's where he was fooled, because watching these *Paramecia* so intently he discovered still a third wrinkle in this process which he called *endomixis*. It's a sort of do-it-yourself conjugation. In endomixis the macronucleus in a *Paramecium* disintegrates, the micronucleus divides, one of those new micronuclei grows up to a new macronucleus and you have a brand new *Paramecium*.

Then there is a fourth process, which is very interesting. It is called *syngamy*. In syngamy two cells fuse to make one; and that, of course, is essentially what happens in sexual reproduction. So, here we have, just among these single-celled organisms, four different ways of going about reproduction but no necessary dying, no corpses.

Let us now take an enormous jump in evolution, to a lower invertebrate, the sea anemone. We've gotten from a single-celled organism to a very many-celled organism. It is not very highly specialized, having only two cell layers where we have three. It has only an ectoderm and endoderm; we also have a mesoderm. It is radially symmetrical, which we think rather primitive compared with our bilateral symmetry, our two-sidedness. Yet this is a big jump from single-celled organisms. The sea anemone splits down the middle, reproducing by simple division, simple fission.

That kind of process is rather a habit at this level of organisms. A close relative, the *Hydra*, reproduces by budding. A bud grows, finally separating from the parent *Hydra*, and that starts some new *Hydras*.

Next we take another enormous jump in the hierarchy of organisms. We have a flatworm named *Planaria*. Such an animal is bilaterally symmetrical as we are. It has three germ layers as we do. It has its nervous system concentrated at the head end. It has rather good sense organs. It represents a big jump from *Hydras* and sea anemones; yet we see this organism reproducing by simple division. It pinches in at the waist and separates into two parts each of which then regenerates whatever it lacks — the tail end cultivates a new head, the head end a new tail, resulting in two brand new flatworms where we started with one. A number of flatworms go through this kind of process. One called Stenotomus breaks into five or six fragments; then each fragment regenrates whatever it lacks.

I thought that with *Planaria* perhaps I had finally found an organism that could just fade away. A Dutch worker named Stoppenbrink many years ago began to starve *Planaria*. As he starved them they began to consume their own substance, following a definite program: First they absorbed whatever sex products there were. Then they went to work on their digestive systems which weren't doing them much good anyhow. Then they started absorbing their muscles. In this way the flatworms got smaller and smaller. The only thing they didn't absorb was the central nervous system; so that as they got smaller and smaller, they came to look highly intellectual — all brain and no worm. By this time I was panting, waiting to read about the moment when Stoppenbrink went into his laboratory, and behold! there were no more flatworms. But to my great disappointment instead he started feeding them again, and they rapidly regenerated everything they had lost. Then, however, Stoppenbrink made a discovery; for what you get back in this way is a brand new flatworm. He found that if you periodically starve flatworms and feed them again, they go on living forever. I am sure that there's a moral in this somewhere.

The furthest I have been able to pursue this way of reproducing by simple division was into the real worms, close relatives of our common earthworm. There is one with a beautiful name, *Enchytraeus fragmentosus*, that has no sex organs at all. It divides entirely by breaking up into many pieces; then each of the pieces regenerates anything it lacks, and one has that many new worms.

But long before this, organisms have taken up a quite different way of reproducing, the sexual mode of reproduction; and it is in the most intimate associations, with the sexual mode of reproduction that death comes upon the scene.

I can describe the situation best in the terms in which a distinguished zoologist of the nineteenth century, August Weismann, described them. Any organism that reproduces sexually begins its life as a single cell, a fertilized egg. The single cell divides repeatedly, eventually to become an adult organism. In the course of its many divisions, there is a line of cells that constitutes what Weismann called the germ line that will eventually produce the mature sex products, eggs or sperm. In the course of those repeated divisions there is also produced a body, what Weismann spoke of as the soma. At sexual maturity this organism mingles its eggs or sperm with the eggs or sperm of a similar adult of the opposite sex; so one has a new fertilized egg, which in exactly the same way, by repeated divisions, produces both sex products and a new body which at maturity, again, mingles its sex products with those of another adult organism. Thus one has the next fertilized egg that by repeated divisions produces the next adult generation. And so on and on, from generation to generation.

On this simple basis August Weismann stated two fundamental principles. The first he spoke of as the *isolation of the germ plasm*. I think the way we would say it now is that genetic information passes always in one direction, always from germ plasm to soma; never in the opposite direction, from soma to germ plasm. That's why there can be no inheritance of acquired characters. An acquired character is a change in the body, in the soma, and there is no way that this can be transmitted into the germ plasm, and hence inherited.

The other principle stated by Weismann he spoke of as the *potential immortality of the germ plasm*. You see, germ plasm goes on making more germ plasm as well as bodies. The line of germ plasm goes on without a break. And now we see what death is. Death is the casting aside of the body, of the soma, after it has done its work. That work is to carry the germ plasm, to feed it, to protect it, to warm it in a warm-blooded organism, and finally to mingle it with the germ plasm of the opposite sex. With that it has completed its function, and can be discarded.

The thought that life is through with the body once sexual reproduction has been accomplished is repugnant to us as men. I shall have more to say of this later. Yet now I should like to say that, repugnant or not, this would be no surprise to a salmon. For in salmon, and eels, and many such creatures, it is all too clear that reproduction is the last act of life, and that the preparation to reproduce is simultaneously the preparation to die.

I should like to speak of one such animal, the lamprey. So-called sea lampreys are probably not familiar to you in the Mid-west, but they are quite familiar to us along the Coasts. That's because of their life cycle. Lampreys have the general shape of eels, and are frequently called lamprey eels, but they are not eels nor are they even fish. They belong to a small group of the most primitive of living vertebrates, the jawless vertebrates or *Agnatha*. They have no jaws, just a sucker disc with a kind of coarse rasp on it. When they get a chance they attach themselves to a fish by that sucker disc, and just begin to rasp their way in. If it is a big enough fish and the fish holds out, the lamprey may end up completely inside of it. A lot of this has been going on in the Great Lakes, as many of you perhaps know, because the digging of a canal per-suaded the lampreys, instead of going down to sea as they had done heretofore, to go into the Great Lakes. For awhile they had almost cleaned out the whole Great Lakes fishery.

The lamprey begins its life as a worm-like larva, with no eyes, buried in the mud or sand of a swift flowing stream. It stays that way for perhaps two or three years. Then it goes through a first metamorphosis, in the course of which, among other things, it acquires eyes. With that it gets itself out from the mud and sand and starts migrating downstream, usually to the sea, where it grows up. At sexual maturity it goes through a second metamor-phosis. There are a lot of changes, but one of the most striking is a complete disintegration of the digestive system. Than animal will never eat again; it loses its entire apparatus for consuming food. Then it starts its journey upstream.

I got my lampreys in the Exeter River in New Hampshire. A hydroelectric development and a dam had been built across the river. The good people of Exeter had been throwing bottles and tin cans into the water below the dam for generations. There wasn't much water and it was pretty perilous, but there were those lampreys still coming up with the first warm days of spring. How they got themselves over the dam I do not know. I suspect they took to the shore, because one of these animals on a sexual migration has only one thing on its mind. It is interested in just one thing, and that is to get up into its spawning ground. There it makes a nest of round stones, the females lay their eggs in the nest, the males shed their sperm over the eggs and with that they're through. All the adult lampreys then die; there is nothing more left in life for them.

The freshwater eels have a life cycle that's just the reverse of that of the lamprey. It was discovered by a great Danish oceanographer, Johannes Schmidt, many years ago. It had been a great mystery until then, where the eels reproduce. The eels of the shores of the Atlantic are of two different species, European and American. All of them come together to spawn in overlapping areas of the Sargasso Sea, the region of the South Atlantic that includes Bermuda. It represents the deepest and saltiest part of the Atlantic Ocean. Having made that enormous journey, the adult eels spawn and die. Then the baby eels make their way back alone. We have no idea how they get back. It takes the American eels about 15 months to come back to our shores, metamorphose, and head upstream. It takes the European eels three years to get back home. There is no record as yet of any baby eel ever getting mixed up and going to the wrong place. When they get into fresh water, they live there for five to fifteen years, growing up. Then at sexual maturity they go through a second metamorphosis. There are a lot of changes: the eyes blow up to twice their former diameter, four times their former area. This animal is getting ready for a deep sea journey. Among other things, there is a complete collapse of the digestive system. Before beginning this enormous journey that will take the adults to the Sargasso Sea, those animals have had their last meal. They will never eat again.

A more familiar organism, the Pacific Coast salmon, has a life cycle like the lamprey. It begins its life invariably in fresh water, grows up a little way, and then goes through a first metamorphosis, losing its spots and nice colors. Up to that point it had looked like a freshwater trout. Now it turns silvery, and goes to sea, where it grows up. At sexual maturity it metamorphoses again, the flesh becomes pink, its color changes. There are all kinds of changes, including again a complete collapse of the digestive system. These salmon, before beginning their migration upstream, are through with eating. They will never eat again. In fact, in many of the males, the jaws become deformed, so that they can no longer meet. This animal isn't interested in jaws any more. In this way it begins its journey upstream. It is no fun. The bears are waiting for it, the Indians are waiting for it, the sportsmen are waiting for it, the canning industry is waiting for it. Those handsome travel folders show you the salmon leaping over falls. That is no fun either. They beat themselves to pieces doing that kind of thing. The salmon that reach the spawning grounds are already dying organisms. They're all torn up with great wounds in their sides which bacteria have invaded. They are capable only of that last act of reproduction, and that's the end of them.

So it is all too clear in these organisms and many others that reproduction is the last act of life; and that the preparation to reproduce is simultaneously the preparation to die.

Sometimes death doesn't wait for the act of reproduction to be accomplished, but takes part in the act. There was a golden period of insect observation in the second half of the nineteenth century. We had Henri Fabre in France, August Forel in Switzerland, Sir John Lubbock in England, and Maurice Maeterlinck in Belgium who wrote about the life of the bee. While these biologists were watching insects so intently, great interest was aroused in the habits of the praying mantis. The praying mantis is a voracious animal. It will tackle something much bigger and stronger than itself, and usually wins. It was observed that when a pair of mantises is copulating, the female, which is a much bigger animal, will occasionally just swing her head around on its beautiful, stalk-like neck and quietly begin to devour the male. He goes right on copulating, while she goes right on eating him. As long as the male's last two abdominal segments are left, they go on copulating.

Some years ago I visited my good friend, Professor Kenneth Roeder at Tufts College. When I got there and asked for him, a student told me, "You'll find Professor Roeder down that hall, last door on the right". So I went down, and there I found Ken Roeder sitting on a soap box watching praying mantises. He offered me another soap box and we sat there, watching together. He told me he had been doing this for years. He told me that, if you've got a female mantis alone in a cage, and put in a male, that male instantly freezes. The praying mantis, like a lot of other animals such as frogs, don't seem to be able to see anything unless it moves. The male knows that, and he's watching the female very carefully. If she looks away for a moment, he takes a hasty few steps forward. Then he freezes again as soon as she looks back. Roeder said that this can go on for hours. If the male is fortunate, he reaches the female, mounts her, and goes through a normal copulation. Incidentally, Roeder told me that once an American male mantis starts copulating, the female never bothers him. It's our better standard of living. But often the female sees him first. With that, she grabs him, always by the head. Then she begins to eat him, always starting with his head. As soon as she has eaten off the head, the male goes into a very interesting pattern of behavior. He plants his front feet squarely and begins to circle around them, meanwhile going through violent copulatory motions. In this way, Roeder told me, such a headless male will frequently succeed in mounting the female and going through a normal copulation.

Ken Roeder is a distinguished neurophysiologist. He was anxious to know that was going on here, and eventually worked that out. There is a copulatory center in the last abdominal segment. But there is an inhibitory center in the subesophageal ganglion that holds the copulatory center in check. It's all very simple. You don't need a female to remove this inhibition. Roeder used a razor blade to cut off the head. Once a male loses his head, the copulatory center is released. So here is an instance in which killing the male helps to stimulate the reproductive act.

At Harvard we have an arrangement whereby undergraduates who feel like and seem to be up to it, can start doing research in their last couple of years. Some years ago a Radcliffe girl came to me to do a senior research. I had just found a few dozen activity cages in the animal room that weren't being used, so I put two and two together, and dreamed up a beautiful problem for that Radcliffe girl.

An activity cage is just a cage in which a rat can live in a little squared-off living compartment that ordinarily has its food and water. He lives there perfectly well, but any time he likes he can go through a little open door into a very carefully balanced running wheel, and can run if he feels like it. When he gets through, he comes back in and eats and generally goes to sleep. When he wakes up, he goes into the wheel and runs a while, and then comes out and eats, and sleeps. That's the way most animals, including rats, go through their day. Such a rat doesn't get anywhere by running. It just does it anyhow. A normal animal is likely to run anything from two to six miles a day.

Life brought me rather early to vitamin A; but sometimes I grow a little restless and want to expand my horizons. So I thought, why not do something with Vitamin B? Just then that Radcliffe girl turned up.

I wasn't going to be reckless, I was going to start with Vitamin B_1, thiamine. Thiamine is an important vitamin. Pharmaceutical houses all over the world have to be ready to estimate how much thiamine is in various foods. I don't know exactly how they go about it now, but in those days they kept big animal rooms full of rats. They would put a group of rats on a thiamine-deficient diet and let them develop rat polyneuritis, which is the rat form of what's called beri-beri in human beings. Every morning a bunch of girls would come in, put on white coats and would go down the line of cages. They would take each rat and would give it the twirl test. They would pick up the rat by the tail, hold it over a table, twirl it and drop it. If you do that with a normal rat, he just gives you a dirty look and runs off; but if you do this with a rat that is beginning to be thiamine deficient — polyneuritic — he has trouble getting his balance back, righting himself again; and that is the first sign of polyneuritis. Once you saw that, you could begin to feed these animals various foods and estimate how much thiamine was in them.

It seemed to me that we could do better than that. I thought that if we took away a rat's thiamine, as it went into polyneuritis, it would of course stop running. That way we would have an early and quantitative sign of thiamine deficiency.

Well, that's where I was fooled. I haven't heard it cited lately, but we used frequently to quote to one another what we called the "Harvard Law of Animal Behavior". It says: under the most rigidly controlled conditions, an animal does as it damn pleases. That's exactly what happened this time. As we took the thiamine away from these rats, instead of stopping running, they just began to run their heads off. They ran day and night, sometimes as much as forty times their normal running. Meanwhile they were losing weight. Occasionally, though we tried to keep that from happening, we'd come in the morning and find a rat dead in the running wheel. The counter would show that somehow it had struggled out a last mile in the previous night.

Well, that seemed extraordinary, and got us pretty excited. So I wondered, how about Vitamin B_2, riboflavin. If you take riboflavin out of the synthetic diet, again the rat begins to run its head off. If you take away its water, the rat runs; if you take its food away, the rat responds by running. If you take away both its food and water — it runs — though you can't keep that up very long and still have a rat. What was going on? All of us are told, usually by someone who is just about to pick our pockets, that self-preservation is the first law of nature. Here were animals going directly counter to that rule. If the animal had just gone to sleep in a corner of its cage, heaven knows what might have happened. The Radcliffe girl might have got married; or we might have just got bored with the experiment. Those animals were just killing themselves.

That made me plunge into the literature; and then I learned that the universal sign of hunger, of genuine deprivation of food, in all animals from protozoa (those single-celled animals) to man, *is increased activity.* You might think, those animals were looking for food. But they're not; they are just driven to run. In the heyday of this kind of experiment, people tried all kinds of things. They took the stomachs out of animals. Your sensation of hunger is just the response to a kind of deep, slow contraction of the upper part of the stomach, called hunger contractions. Those animals behaved just like the others. One could take the cerebral cortex out of an animal. Such an animal was incapable of recognizing food; yet when it was hungry, it ran. It couldn't feed itself, but if you poked food into its mouth, it swallowed and so was fed. Then it would go to sleep, then it would wake up and run until it was fed again, after which it would go to sleep. Our rats weren't looking for food. Such a hungry animal is not asked to run, it is *told* to run. These are orders, not requests. They are forced to run.

I think that what we have here is a kind of small scale model for a well known phenomenon, a hunger migration. The most famous of the hunger migrations, one that all of you've heard about, are the migrations of the lemmings. The lemmings are rodents that live high up on the mountainsides in Norway. There is a mythology about this that says that in a lemming year the lemmings come down from the mountains in hundreds of thousands if not millions, and go rampaging through the cities, driving people indoors, stopping all of the traffic. They're on their way to the ocean. When they reach the ocean they plunge in, and in an act of mass suicide, swim off and are never seen again.

Well, it isn't quite that way. Lemmings are rather cute looking but unsociable organisms. A lemming ordinarily will tolerate no more than one other lemming of the opposite sex. When a pair of these, traveling together, meets another such pair they sort of growl at each other and each pair goes its way. Norway is of such a shape that for animals wandering off the mountainsides, many of them reach the sea; and it is true that many of them then go into the water and swim off never to be seen again. But they were not searching out the sea. The lemmings on the other side of the same mountains in the same way reach the plains of Lapland, and go wandering off across those plains to die.

That is the point. It's pretty well realized by now that that kind of migration is impelled by hunger. It happens in a population that has outgrown its resources. Animals are hungry, and a hungry animal has to run. It's driven to run. It isn't looking for anything. It just has to keep moving. You might think that the point of such a hunger migration is colonization. You might think such a horde of hungry animals leaving their home territory are looking for a better place to live. But there is no such place. If there were a better place to live, they would have found it long before. There is no place for them. The point of a hunger migration is not to colonize, but to remove the migrating animals. The end of every hunger migration is the death of the migrating animals.

Some of you may wonder why I include men in this pattern. You may say, "Well, I don't run around when I'm hungry". That's because you are said to be civilized. That gets in the way of all kinds of sensible patterns. If you want to see men behaving this way you have to catch them in the raw.

One way to do that is to observe an infant. Every young couple knows what it's like with a new infant. It is just the classic animal pattern. A new infant wakes up, starts to writhe, and yells its head off and grows red in the face, and is full of activity. Every muscle is working. Then you start feeding it. Usually it falls asleep in the middle of the feeding. You have to keep patting its bottom just to get it to finish feeding. Then it sleeps awhile, then it wakes up, writhes and yells and has to be fed again. That's the way it starts its life; until that young couple civilizes it into eight hours on and eight hours off.

The other way to catch human beings in the raw is when they're asleep. There was a golden period that I look back upon with great regret, in which the cheapest of experimental animals were medical students. Graduate students were even better. In the old days if you offered a graduate student a thiamine-deficient diet, he gladly went on it, for that was the only way he could eat. Science is getting to be more and more difficult.

Some years ago, in the laboratory of Professor Curt Richter at Johns Hopkins, he offered a group of medical students the extraordinary privilege of a bed in the laboratory. There were a few formalities. Before the medical student got into bed, he swallowed a balloon attached to a rubber tube that came out of his mouth and went to a mercury manometer which recorded through the night the motions of his stomach. Then that cot was not an ordinary cot. It was very carefully balanced, so that if that medical student moved in his sleep, that was all recorded on a revolving drum. Well, in just the classical pattern, in a four-hour cycle right through the night, the medical student's stomach would begin to go through the slow, deep hunger contractions. As they reached their peak, the medical student began to toss around in his bed. Then the hunger contractions would die down, and the medical student go back to sleeping quietly, until four hours later he went through the same cycle.

As for a human hunger migration, there is a beautiful passage in Herodotus' *Histories* which has it in classic form. Herodotus is describing the origin of the Greek games, what we now call the Olympic Games. He says that in the reign of Atys, son of Manes, there was a great famine in Lydia. It persisted year after year. After seven years the king ruled that all the people must spend every second day in athletic games and on alternate days they would eat. After seven years of this, the famine still persisting, the king divided the population in half, half to migrate, the other half to remain. That brings us at last to man.

It's rather odd that we regard mass suicide on the part of lem-

mings as an aberration, as a kind of psychopathic behavior; whereas our way of dealing with the same problem is considered normal.
Where the lemmings go off to die, we go off to kill; for it's equally
true for the human migrants that there is no other place for them.
Every place is occupied. Have you ever heard of people migrating
to a place fit to live where there were no people before? There are
always people. If the migration ends in a colonization, that's
through conquest. It is strange that we look on that as normal and
proper, whereas the lemmings seem to be doing something aber-
rant; for biologically there is much to be said for the way lemmings go about it.

On the one hand, the way the lemmings do it, there is a mini-
mum of dying. As soon as enough lemmings have left the center of
population, there is enough food for those that remain, so the
migration automatically stops. Second, there is no destruction.
The lemmings' home territory is just as good as it ever was. Third,
and whenever I say this I shudder, since I can't jump over my
shadow, but a selection process is at work. It's the hungriest lemmings that go off to die; the ones that are doing better stay home.
Whereas in the human way of doing things, we pick the flower of
our manhood to go off to kill and die. The lemmings are exercising
better biology.

I would like to return now to the repugnant thought that life is
through with animals once reproduction has been accomplished.
It's not true for man. To relieve this situation of the usual Polly-
anna practice in which, whenever one describes something uncomfortable, one explains that it's not true for us, let me talk about
bees. All of you know that the heart of what goes on in a bee
colony is what is done by the workers. The workers build the hive;
they take care of the young, they forage for food, they clean the
hive, they run the air-conditioning system, everything. They do
everything; and yet they are sexless females that have no part in
reproduction. The only sexual female in the hive is the queen. And
that's the point. If animals such as bees have a society, then indiv-

iduals can serve the purposes of that society, and whether they reproduce or not becomes irrelevant. We human beings have a society, and that's the way it is with us. Beethoven, so far as we know, had no children; Bach had a lot of them. Who cares? That isn't the reason we go to Beethoven and Bach. Rembrandt had one boy; Isaac Newton had no children. Who cares? It's completely irrelevant. For organisms that have a society this becomes a complete irrelevance.

Since we have had a history, men have pursued an ideal of immortality. I am speaking now, not of immortality of the soul (I don't really know what that means), but of fleshly immortality, of immortality of the body. Over the centuries and the millenia, one has searched for the Philosopher's Stone, the Fountain of Youth, all of those efforts somehow to abolish death.

That age-old quest for fleshly immortality is a hoax. Peter Medawar has a book called *The Uniqueness of the Individual*, and in its first two chapters you will find this all laid out. Peter Medawar points out that if we already possessed every feature of bodily immortality that one could want, it would change our present state very little. On examination it would turn out to offer us nothing. As Medawar says, we'd all like to grow up, so let's be able to reach something like 20 years of age, and then never grow any older. Then he adds: let there be no natural death. Medawar says that at that point he got worried, and went about asking all his physician friends in London whether they had ever seen a person die of old age. All of us go about with the familiar concept of death of old age, of natural death. It turned out that none of the doctors he knew had ever observed it. I think if a physician wrote on a death certificate that old age was the cause of death, he'd be thrown out of the union. There is always some final event, some failure of an organ, some last attack of pneumonia, that finishes off a life. No one dies of old age. Nevertheless, said Medawar, no natural death; and then he said, "Let's give them a bonus of perpertual fertility." No matter how long this person lived, he'd be as fertile as at age twenty. That's about all one could ask for, isn't it?

Medawar points out that with all these conditions fulfilled, our lives would have changed very little, that is if one went on living human lives, the way we are used to living them. Every time you cross a street you risk your life; there are cars, trucks, trains, and planes; there are viruses and bacteria. They need to live, too, and they'd be working away still. There are electric circuits, and all the other hazards. All the insurance actuaries would have to do is hang around for awhile, and pretty soon they'd send you the new rates. Matters would have changed so little, says Medawar, that possibly our patterns of old age and death are essentially following the inevitable patterns, were we, in fact, immortal.

The strangest thing is that we *have* immortality, but in the wrong place. We have it in the germ plasm; we want it in the soma, in the body. We have fallen in love with the body. That's that thing that looks back at us from the mirror. That's the repository of that lovely identity that you keep chasing all your life. And as for that potentially immortal germ plasm, where that is one hundred years, one thousand years, ten thousand years hence, hardly interests us.

I used to think that way, too, but I don't any longer. You see, every creature alive on the earth today represents an unbroken line of life that stretches back to the first primitive organism to appear on this planet; and that is about three billion years. That really *is* immortality. For if that line of life had ever broken, how could we be here? All that time, our germ plasm has been living the life of those single-celled creatures, the protozoa, reproducing by simple division, and occasionally going through the process of syngamy — the fusion of two cells to form one — in the act of sexual reproduction. All that time that germ plasm has been making bodies and casting them off in the act of dying. If the germ plasm wants to swim in the ocean, it makes itself a fish; if the germ plasm wants to fly in the air, it makes itself a bird. If it wants to go to

Gustavus Adolphus College, it makes itself a man. The strangest thing of all is that the germ plasm that we carry around within us has done all those things. There was a time, hundreds of millions of years ago, when it was making fish. Then at a later time it was making amphibia, things like salamanders; and then at a still later time it was making reptiles. Then it made mammals, and now it's making men. If we only have the restraint and good sense to leave it alone, heaven knows what it will make in ages to come.

I, too, used to think that we had our immortality in the wrong place, but I don't think so any longer. I think it's in the right place. I think that is the only kind of immortality worth having — and we have it.

U.S. VON EULER

Physiological aspects of aging and death

Dr. ULF von EULER was born in Stockholm in 1905. He originally intended to enter the field of engineering but transferred to the Royal Caroline Institute to obtain his M.D. in 1930. He then began a brilliant career as a teacher and research scientist at the Royal Caroline Institute that was to lead him to a Nobel Prize in Medicine in 1970.

His research in the area of the sympathetic nervous system led to an understanding of the actions of many drugs in cardiology, psychiatry and neurology. L-dopa, one of the well-known drugs for the treatment of Parkinson's disease, is a direct outgrowth of this basic research on the sympathetic nervous system.

Dr. von Euler is the son of two distinguished Swedish scientists. His father, Hans von Euler, received the Nobel Prize in chemistry in 1929 when he was director of the Chemical Institute at the University of Stockholm. His mother, Astrid Cleve, was also a prominent scientist.

He has received honorary doctorates from distinguished universities in six different countries, France, Germany, Sweden, Belgium, Brazil and Argentina. He has received several international awards in the science field. In 1965 he was elected president of the Nobel Foundation Board, a position he still holds.

The topic set for this year's Nobel Conference, while forming a logical continuation of the issues brought forward in previous conferences, presents a large variety of problems which have challenged the minds of mankind since early days. The opinions of laymen and scientists alike may differ on almost every single point depending on the partly self-selected programming of the mental machinery. Unfortunately there are very few criteria which would allow a decision as to whether one or the other interpretation of the available alternatives is to be given preference and should be used as a basis for further thought or action. Thus the general issue "end of life", taken in the meaning of purpose and goal, has been subject to much consideration and philosophical speculation and clearly offers a variety of possibilities. Even if no final answer can be given, the formulation of alternatives represents mental exercise of high priority.

For a biologist it is always tempting to observe the life pattern of other living organisms and try to obtain support in this way for one or the other of these alternatives. Basically this procedure suffers from the methodological weakness of being in principle a kind of extrapolation, which always has to be used with great care. On the other hand the gradual development of the structural basis for mental activity as displayed in animal species at varying levels of achievement, leading up to the human being, may cautiously be applied as a basis for considering the problems in question. One of the main points, admittedly, in this context, is whether the ability of man to speak and write constitutes such a fundamental new quality that similarities in other manifestations of life and behaviour appear relatively less significant. If one believes that the human species is unique in another sense than for instance a fox or a whale, then the interpretation of human life problems will be infinitely more difficult, complex, and perhaps elude final conclusions, like other isolated phenomena. If, on the other hand, one chooses to regard human vital forces and manifestations as a link in a continuous biological chain which, although somewhat irregular, is open to inspection, studies and evaluation, then the prospects are brighter and we may have a moderately firm foundation for a consideration of life which might be used to our advantage. A conceptual basis of this kind will then form a branch of life sciences, distinguishing it from concepts based largely or exclusively on endogenous mental processes which perhaps might yield results more like those derived from a self-programming computer.

Many warnings have, with a certain justification, been issued against the application of results won in extrahuman beings on the conditions valid for man. Every worker in life sciences knows the lurking criticism that results obtained on animals may not hold for man. If this is true for physiology in general it must necessarily apply also to the mental processes. But if we accept, as is often done, that a large number of vital processes are in their fundamentals rather similar in animals and man this would probably also apply to mental functions including behaviour and sociology. The question which then immediately presents itself is whether we know sufficient about the forces which determine these parameters of life in animals. Despite considerable efforts and remarkable results in certain areas, it is my opinion that the question should be answered in the negative. The majority of people still feel alienated to large groups of animal species and we are far from extending the present trend to include all human beings as our brethren to the concept that all living creatures form, biologically speaking, a big family. The reasons for this discrimination are many: practical, esthetical, competitive and others, but to a large extent this aspect has been prevented by the old idea of man's superiority and relative uniqueness. An entirely new view on this problem may be warranted but is hardly likely to come very soon. An altered biological attitude may not provide an answer to the question of purpose or goal of life, but it may help to eliminate some of the more fanciful concepts. A wide latitude of individual ideas is likely to persist in this matter.

Taking a holobiotic view of the life phenomena to be observed in the animal kingdom, a number of secondary problems appear, holding many practical implications. Some of them have a slight academic touch but constitute nevertheless, or perhaps because of this, a challenge to the analytical power of the human mind. Many attempts have thus been made to give definitions of life and death. Increased insight into the aging process with all its inherent theoretical and practical consequences is further indispensable for a useful discussion of the present topic. A good understanding of these dynamic problems will no doubt be of value for mankind as a whole and may possibly eliminate or reduce disturbance and agony of various kinds, if applied in an appropriate way.

Definitions of life have been formulated in many different ways and I do not intend to give a comprehensive picture of this theme with variations. If we speak of active life and leave aside temporary dormant or passive life, the physiologist may find self-regulated metabolism one of the main features. The homeostasis concept, as formulated by physiologists, constitutes one of the fundamental principles of life. This includes intake of material and removal of waste. Mobility is another side issue. More basically important, again, is reparation or regeneration which is truly a main feature of life.

Another process which characterizes life is aging and its logical corollary, a limited life span. If we are to talk of life in general and not as a temporary phenomenon, it requires reproduction or replication in order to make up for the losses. From these points of view one might regard metabolism, regulated by homeostasic mechanisms, regeneration, and aging, as primary features of life, perpetuated and supported by reproduction, mobility, signal systems, growth, and exchange of matter with the ambient materia.

In order to fulfill these functions the matter is structurally organized in the cell. We can hardly conceive life in a free-flowing system. The metabolic aspect of life has been formulated as an open system characterized by a dynamic equilibrium with the ambient materia, maintaining an organization which is not subject to entropy in the physical sense. In order to maintain this equilibrium various homeostatic systems are used, primarily utilizing the feed-back principle (Bertalanffy, 1966).

The problem of defining life has more recently obtained an interesting twist, namely in attempts to demonstrate extra-terrestrial life (cf. Eugster, 1969). Against the background given above it is clear that a variety of methods can be used for detection of life. Metabolism will offer a series of parameters where present techniques offer high sensitivity. Since metabolic processes as a rule are accompanied by a release of heat, this may be measured. Reproduction can likewise be measured e.g. in bacteria, often by growth. Chemically, the occurrence of a specific optical isomer is a characteristic sign of life. The same is true for enzymes. In the latest years several sophisticated techniques have been described for automatic sampling and detection of life.

One of the fundamental facts in animal biology is the limited life-span. This must be accepted as a basic feature and its statistically average length is an integrative part in the life system to which we belong. This should be accepted as perfectly natural and should be recognized as such under all circumstances. But this is by far not the case. It may have been regarded in this way in more primitive stages of human development, but as concepts have become more and more diversified in connection with the ever increasing use of words, various new ideas began to form themselves. Some of these found more resonance than others in receptive human minds and so the concept of reincarnation or eternal life became widely embraced. This concept was probably accepted by many as taking some of the edge out of death and allowing the thought that death only appears as a temporary endpoint.

It is sometimes said that aging begins at birth. Our knowledge about the alterations of somatic and mental nature which constitute aging is, to say the least, incomplete, and the definition of aging accordingly complex and difficult.

First we have to consider in this context what may be termed the normal life-span. This is a biological constant, characteristic for each species. For man it has been estimated at a little over 80 years on an average. Granting biological variations one will find value statistically deviating in both directions. What is definitely established, however, is that during the last century an increasing proportion of the population reaches the 'normal life-span'. While in 1870 only about 15% of the recorded deaths in a representative material reached this level, an increase to about 60% was noted in 1950. The estimated 'normal life-span' does not seem to have changed significantly in the last 2000 years. It has been assumed, however, that man in the future not only will differ from the present type in various somatic respects, but also reach a higher age.

Observations on unicellular organisms indicate that life continues over long periods even if cell division is prevented. Even isolated organs from warm-blooded animals can survive for a surprisingly long time as shown by the perfused chicken heart which was kept alive for 28 years in Carrel's experiments.

It is interesting in this context to note that certain plants can continue to live as an entity for several thousand years through a dynamic process of cell division and apposition of new tissue, although these processes show a recession with time.

In plants as well as in animals it is notable that different kinds of cells have a different life-span. An example of a fixed average age is the life-span or eryhrocytes, which is of the order of one month.

In animals the life-spans vary from a few days in certain insects up to over 100 years for the giant turtle. In general it can be said that aging is a constant feature in those species which lack the ability to regenerate nerve cells. This is particularly the case when the species contain a more developed central nervous system.

In the plants it has been assumed that auxins and auxin oxidase represent chemical factors responsible for aging. Is it possible that some well defined chemical has a central role also in the aging of animals?

From the point of view of gerontology man lives too long and the processes of aging are too slow for experimental purposes even if experimenting were allowed. The classical animal for such studies is the rat which lives about 2·5 years and becomes markedly senile at 2 years of age.

Aging has been described by philosophers and authors in illustrative and adequate terms although mostly in other words than those used by the life scientist. From a scientific point of view it is of importance to describe the time course of aging and its mechanisms. In general it can be said that aging before 20, or progeria, is genetically determined, whereas aging before 50 (proterogeria) as a rule has exogenous causes. Aging at 60 is constitutional (eugeria) and if it occurs after 60 it is delayed (diatrigeria), again on a genetical basis.

Gerontological research has directed its interest both to structural, physiological and biochemical phenomena in order to describe and characterize the changes which occur. These are not running parallel in different tissues and organs. Thus it is well known that the brain undergoes a continuous reduction in the number of cells, a kind of involution or atropy which becomes marked after 50 years of age. The total loss of weight amounts to about 250 g or about 20% of the maximal weight. Assuming a number of brain cells of 12 billions, this corresponds to a loss of roughly 100 000 cells per day after 20 years of age. A certain shift in the proportions of brain neurons and glia occurs, as well as of lipids and proteins.

The overt changes in the structure of the skin are well known, particularly the loss of elasticity, and also changes in the colour of the hair. The respiratory system becomes less efficient, and it is said that the old individual is living under conditions corresponding to those of a middle-aged person at an altitude of 6000 ft. The reproductive organs diminish their activity as evidenced by the ovarial involution at around 50 years in the female. In the male the reproductive pattern shows wider variations.

With advancing technology and improved means for medical care important changes have gradually come into play as regards the course of the terminal period of life. While life in former days not seldom ended abruptly as a result of trauma and disease, it is now often possible to delay the endpoint of life, sometimes to a considerable extent. This, however, has created a number of new problems of a medical, psychological, social and economic nature. Thus an increasing number of citizens will require the aid of individuals or institutions, hospitals, and homes for aged people, mainly because of reduced mobility, incontinence or psychic disturbances. As a result a large number of aged people who are not capable of maintaining an acceptable life have to rely on other individuals. This has, somewhat cynically, been termed "the survival of the unfittest". In our time it is almost axiomatic that sick and aged people should have all the possible medical care available, but it is easy to imagine that in the future a very large number of citizens will be kept alive for periods which tend to increase as the tools of the medical profession become more effective. Obviously this will create problems of various kinds.

Some of the many practical implications incurred by the terminal stage, which may extend from months to years, have recently been discussed by a group of scientists and have led to coining of the term pre-death (Isaacs et al., 1971). There is every reason to believe that this will develop into a major socio-medical problem with an inherent tendency to bind an increasing portion of the resources of society and to engage a growing number of man-hours. The mere raising of the scientific question of whether a continuation of the present principles for treatment is biologically sound might be considered appallingly heretical today, but still it may have to turn up in the future for technical and practical reasons.

Are there any alternatives? Any deviation from the commonly accepted lines of thought requires, as everybody knows, independence of mind and, in addition, a lot of courage to formulate or express. This was true for Galilei in the 17th century, for Semmelweiss in the 19th century, and is certainly not less true today. It is therefore a striking event when a philosopher of reputation makes a plea for what he calls suicide clinics. We are admittedly shocked at first by the idea but it might still be objectively considered.

The idea has recently been developed in Denmark by H.C. Seierup and commented upon by Ingemar Hedenius, Professor of Philosophy at the University of Uppsala. His first point is that suicide belongs to the human rights. He points out that since suicide is considered highly honorable when applied during a war in order to promote victory, it is difficult to regard it as shameful in other situations. If suicide is acceptable when in the interest of the state it should also be allowed for the individual.

The idea behind the proposal of suicide clinics is that this would allow individuals who find their lives unbearable to receive advice and suitable means for ending that life. According to the proponents, this should also prevent some unnecessary suicides, in cases where an individual might find advice and care leading to a return to life.

Clearly this concept is complicated by a large number of factors which may jeopardize its materialization, even if it is accepted as such. The concept of suicide as a legitimate way of ending life should, however, be considered and discussed in the same objective way as other problems, free from the barriers set by ingrown, conventional ways of thinking. It should also be remembered that suicide was a common method of ending life in older days, at least among some populations.

The general issue, as discussed by the philosopher, can also be applied to a more specific problem — the right of suicide during severe illness, intractable pain, and during a protected period of weakness preceding death. The objections to this right have been more eagerly discussed than the indisputable right itself. The ideological barrier has undoubtedly caused much prolongation of pain and unhappiness for the sick individual as well as for his dependents. By occupying a bed for a life he deems as useless, a severely ill person may even prevent some other individual from receiving useful care.

In this context it is perhaps of interest to note that similar thoughts were not alien to Alfred Nobel, who on various occasions had expressed the idea of a kind of "suicide home" in Paris for individuals who wished to depart from this life with dignity and without pain, instead of having to "drown themselves in the dirty water of the Seine". Even if the idea of a "suicide institute" might be regarded as some kind of grim intellectual sport in Nobel, the mere mentioning of it to various acquaintances and friends indicates that the thought had dwelled in Nobel's mind (Sohlman, 1962).

From this point the step is not very distant to the much-debated problem of euthanasia. Even if subserving the same purpose to shorten pain and relieve unhappiness and anguish, euthanasia is in principle quite different and its implications much more multifaceted.

The sociology and psychology of dying and death have attracted a growing interest in the last 10—20 years as evidenced by numerous articles, books and conferences on the subject (cf. Kubler—Ross, 1971, "Meaning of death"). Still it has to be admitted that preparation and training even of doctors and health personnel for meaningful actions in this field has not yet been adequately developed. Noteworthy attempts have been made, however, not least in this country. The main goal is to assist the terminally sick patient to what has been termed "the appropriate death" (Weisman and Hackett, 1961) or ortothanasia (Eissler, 1955). A prerequisite for any successful attempt in this direction is motivation from the patient. In certain cases religious or philosophical support will be most helpful, and the psychiatrist should help to establish such contacts as might be of greatest value to the patient. It must not be forgotten, however, that any treatment of a really helpful nature requires a certain amount of mental strength and cooperation from the patient's side. It is the experience of the psychiatrist that a certain number of the patients are aware of the fact that they approach death, even if this is not expressed verbally. It is sometimes maintained that the patient has the right to know whether he is approaching death but it is equally important to realize that the patient has the right not to want to know (Feigenberg, 1971).

In many patients there is an element of hope in spite of a situation which should not warrant this. It is probably in some way related to the idea of eternal life. The experienced psychologist or psychiatrist has a complex pattern to consider and to utilize for the benefit of his patient. He must be able technically to cope with a multitude of emotional factors, such as defence mechanisms, anxiety, aggressiveness and depression, often combined. It is easy to imagine how difficult this task is, since different individuals may react entirely differently, depending on previous programming, exogenous and endogenous, of their mental life.

Literature is full of descriptions of how different individuals meet death, and there is little doubt that intellectually active people take influence from the evaluations presented by the authors. In this way a kind of idealized pattern will emerge, which may even serve as a means of support and guidance. For other groups death comes as a natural thing, not influenced by a literary bias; it comes more biologically plain as it were, as observed and often admirably described both in prose and verse. Even the thought of a decent funeral can be a source of satisfaction during the terminal period. It should be recalled that funerals, especially in some rural districts, comprise both elements of a ceremonial—religious character and of a more worldly type which does not exclude a moderate and decent hilarity, which appears to represent a natural compensatory device.

In this way some of the inevitable sadness of death is relieved, both for the dying individual and for those who stand to mourn. A balanced resignation will then become the prevalent feeling.

Another factor which sometimes in a natural way contributes to making death less painful is the continuous change in the ambient life, sociological, ideological, economical and in other respects. Particularly in the aged it is doubtful whether they in general perceive the ambient world as moving towards a better state. On the contrary it is quite common that old people think and speak of the good old days and have difficulty in identifying themselves as members of the current society. This reduces the feeling of fear of death.

To find a formula which would fit all situations when a medical man is confronted with the question of whether he should allow a sick patient to die, or make every effort to prolong his life, is hardly possible. If euthanasia were legally permitted under certain circumstances, this would bring a new principle in action which would involve many hazards. It is therefore natural that the majority of doctors seem to oppose the idea of euthanasia (Biörck, 1968). It could easily lead to a growing lack of confidence in the doctors. It has been argued that it is better if the patient can rest completely assured that the doctor will do everything he can to prolong life, even if the patient would like to terminate it. The negative side of this is that the patient will have few opportunities to do so in a way that would not cause criticism directed towards the hospital care and supervision. It is also doubtful whether a strict border-line can be kept between active and passive euthanasia. When it is generally realized and admitted that modern medical care possesses highly efficient weapons to fight death and prolong suffering, the attitude towards euthanasia, especially the passive kind, may change and become more permissive.

If the patient clearly expresses his wish to be allowed to terminate his life, should he be denied this right? A doctor could almost always make the necessary arrangements for himself if he so wishes but why should the layman be in a different position? Let us hope that the future will find a solution acceptable to all individuals. It could well be based on the words of Irvine Page (1962) of Cleveland Clinic who wrote:

"Is death to be looked upon as evil? Cannot man have confidence in the orderliness of nature − that death, like birth, will be painless and is not to be feared? In our desperate attempts to prolong life, we are, I think, losing sight of these simple ideas.

A man should still have the right to die at home among those he loves. All reasonable efforts should be made to stay death, but there are unreasonable limits as well. The decision to keep the body alive after it has irretrievably failed should, if possible, I believe, rest solely on the desires of the individual. Most people need never make the decision. Let us not forget that they must be given the right to die with dignity. Socrates knew that nothing can harm a good man either in life or after death, and his fortunes are not a matter of indifference to the gods. Life cannot be replaced by the artificial. Death cannot be averted by a substitute."

References

American Association for the Advancement of Science, 137th meeting, Dec. 1970, Chicago, Ill. *Problems in the meaning of death.*
Barghoorn, E.S. and J.W. Schopf, Microorganisms three billion years old from the Precambrian of South Africa. *Science* 1966, *152*, 758−763.
Bertalanffy, L. v., *Bild der Wissenschaft* 1966, No. 9, p. 716.
Biörck, G., *Thought of Life and Death*, Perspectives in Biology and Medicine, 1968, *11*, 527−543.

Carrel, A., *Berlin. Klin. Wschr.*, 1931, 24.

Eissler, 1965, Quoted from Feigenberg (1971).

Eugster, J., *Die Forschung nach ausserirdischem Leben* (Zurich: Orell Fussli Verlag, 1969).

Feigenberg, L., Människovärdig död, *Läkartidningen* 1971, *68*, 5965—5975.

Hedenius, I., Kliniker for sjalvmord, *Dagens Nyheter* 1971, Dec. 14.

Isaacs, B., J. Gunn, A. McKechan, I. McMillan and Y. Neville, The concept of pre-death, *The Lancet*, 1971, May 29, 1115—1119.

Kubler-Ross, E., *On Death and Dying* (Macmillan, 1971).

Luth, P., Alterforschung und Altersbehandlung, *Wissenschaftl. Berichte* 2, E. Merck, Darmstadt.

Page, I., Death with Dignity, *Modern Medicine*, 1962, Oct.

Simpson, K., Moment of death, *Abbottempo in Review*, 1970, p. 78, Abbott Universal Ltd.

Sirtori, C., The New Frontiers of Science, *Perspectives in Biology and Medicine*, 1970, *13*, 231—254.

Sohlman, R., in: *Nobel the Man and His Prizes* (Amsterdam: Elsevier Publishing Co., 1962) p. 36.

Weisman and Hackett, 1961, Quoted from Feigenberg (1971).

Nathan A. SCOTT, Jr.

*The modern imagination of death**

* Portions of this material have been adapted from my book *The Broken Center: Studies in the Theological Horizon of Modern Literature* (New Haven: Yale University Press, 1966), with the permission of the Yale University Press.

DR. NATHAN A. SCOTT, Jr., was born in Cleveland in 1925. He was educated at the University of Michigan (A.B. 1944), Union Theological Seminary in New York City (B.D.) and Columbia University (Ph.D. 1949). He is an ordained priest of the Episcopal Church.

He started his career as dean of the chapel at Virginia Union University before moving to Howard University where he taught in the humanities. In 1955 he moved to the Divinity School of the University of Chicago as assistant professor of theology and literature. Since 1964 he has held the rank of professor. He is the author of more than a dozen books covering a wide range in religion and literature. One of his volumes is entitled *The Modern Vision of Death* (1967). He also is co-editor of the Journal of Religion.

Dr. Scott is a fortunate replacement for Sweden's poet Harry Martinson who was forced to cancel his appearance at this conference in mid-December because of a family accident.

Dr. Scott was the Hill Family Foundation Visiting Lecturer at Gustavus during the spring semester of 1954. His brilliance of mind and clarity of thought exhibited during those weeks on campus earned him the admiration of all the faculty and students.

It was, I think, rather a bold venture for those who were planning this year's Nobel Conference here at Gustavus Adolphus College to insist that we come together for the sake of thinking about what is the most ultimate emergency of human life — namely, the emergency that looms ahead for all men in the certainty that they must eventually die. And I'm led to speak of the boldness with which the central theme of the Conference was conceived, because, for all of the radical pressure which it must in the nature of the case exert upon the human spirit, there is perhaps no other great theme of human existence before which the people of our age are so incompetent as they are in the presence of death. Man has, of course, no doubt always been reduced to a strange kind of stuttering and stammering in the face of his last enemy, but I suspect that in no previous age have men sought to avoid so desperately as they do in our own time any forthright confrontation with the fact of our mortality. We shun the old, and our odd funeral customs are all calculated to persuade us that the dead are not really dead after all. Yet everywhere in this century we have heard, as Helmut Kuhn says, "the clicking and grating of spades" [1] — and, in a time that has known the obscenity of gas chambers and concentration camps, of lampshades nicely contrived of human skin and soap manufactured of human fat, and that does at last descry the holocaustal glow of the great mushroom in the skies — in such a time we feel ourselves, all of us, to be a generation of "grave-diggers at work". And most especially, of course, these past few years death has leapt out at us in a strangely melodramatic and

---

[1] Helmut Kuhn, *Encounter with Nothingness: An Essay on Existentialism* (Chicago: Henry Regnery Co., 1949), p. 82.

disquieting way – John and Robert Kennedy, Martin Luther King, Biafra, Pakistan, the whole tragedy of Vietnam. The events, in other words, of the days through which we have lived have put us very deeply in mind of what the late Albert Camus called "the cruel mathematics that command our condition". So the most sober people begin, with a new kind of disenchanted clarity, to be aware of the time in which man dwells as the time of the hour-glass, and they are often to be found meditating now in various ways on the fact that, as Dylan Thomas says, though we sing in our chains like the sea, Time holds us green and dying. We look out upon the global insecurity and hazard of human existence in our period, and, inevitably, there is borne in upon us a deepened sense of how fragile, of how vulnerable, of how impermanent, the human thing really is. And thus we are often wondering today what it means to die.

Now my own assignment in this Conference is that of reviewing something of the testimony about the meaning of death that emerges from the great literature of our period. And since our way of understanding death is but a special case of the more general way in which we understand the nature of time and its transiency, it has occurred to me that perhaps the best method of defining the sense of death in modern literature is one that will do so by way of some analysis of the general sense of time which this literature evinces.

The literature of the twentieth century is, of course, a literature obsessed with time, with time lost and time recaptured, with time as duration and time as disintegration: and most of the major poems and plays and novels of our period prove, on examination, to be various kinds of metaphors on the nature of time.

I suppose our modern fascination with time has perhaps its most immediate root in the sheer crowdedness of the time that we experience today in the Western world. For, as a result of all the marvellous techniques of modern communication that bring Washington and London and Paris and Moscow into such close proximity, it is possible today for an event, as it were, to be *instantly* recorded by our newspapers and radio and television networks. We live in an age in which there is no longer any real interim between the happening of a significant occurrence and its being learned about all across the globe. And, as a result, we doubtless some- times feel that radio and television and the press are actually en- gaged in a mass-production of events, so much do we feel the surfaces of our lives to be overpopulated with events. Think, for example, of the kind of experience that we have when we leaf through the pages of so characteristic a phenomenon of our cul- ture as *Life* Magazine. As one looks at "Jesus freaks" performing their devotions in Los Angeles, at scenes of the deepening agony in Northern Ireland, at some new American enormity in Vietnam, at Jacqueline and Aristotle Onassis romping on the island of Skor- pios, at a fancy house-party perhaps for the Jet Set somewhere in Connecticut — isn't it the case, as one leafs through the pages of something like *Life* Magazine, that one has the feeling of being flicked at, as if one were watching an old silent movie. And, in a way, the whole of contemporary life is very much like an early cinema show: the sensation that is everywhere felt is that of being flicked at: the surfaces of our lives are felt to be overpopulated by reason of the sheer mass-production of events in the modern world.

Now it is this crowdedness of time that gives rise in our age to a special sort of dizziness: we have the sense that *all* time is some- how eternally present, that all the fragments of all possible exper- ience are somehow simultaneously co-existent in the present. And everything appears to be whirling into everything else.

Whereas life once appeared to be a pilgrimage and like a jour- ney, it now seems to be very much like one of our major airports on a busy holiday week end. And thus it is indeed that the time which modern men characteristically experience is very much like that of the cinema. In the cinema, time tends very often to lose its uninterrupted continuity: in close-ups, it can be brought to a standstill; it can be reversed in flash-backs; it can be skipped across in visions of the future; simultaneous events can be shown successively, and temporally distinct events can be shown simultaneously, by double-exposures and alternations. And it is just the kind of irregularity belonging to cinematic time that seems to form a large part of the distinctively modern experience.

So, since the tempo of human life in our period leads men to experience time as scattered and fluid, inevitably there arises the anxious surmise that there may be nothing any longer that can be counted on to hold time together, to order it and stabilize it and give it firm anchorage. Which is to say that Eternity is felt to be in eclipse: for time has lost all coherence: one instant is indistinguishable from another or is merely engulfed by another, and all moments seem to have fallen into a strange kind of impoverishment and mediocrity.

We should not, therefore, find it surprising that modern literature does not record the kind of concern that was generally expressed in earlier periods whenever time was the subject of reflection. The Psalmist often thinks, for example, about how

> .... we spend our years as a tale that is told. The days of our years are threescore years and ten; and if by reason of strength they be fourscore years, yet is their strength labour and sorrow; for it is soon cut off, and we fly away.

And this is in line with the reminder in Shakespeare's *Cymbeline* that

> Golden lads and girls all must,
> As chimney-sweepers, come to dust —

or with Wordsworth's reflection in the "Immortality" Ode that

> The Clouds that gather round the setting sun
> Do take a sober colouring from any eye
> That hath kept watch o'er man's mortality ....

But, though this traditional kind of dirge on the mortality of the human creature is something which still persists in modern literature, it has long since ceased being a characteristic emphasis. For the drama of our life in time is very often felt now to be itself a kind of death: time itself is felt to be hopelessness and homesickness and abandonment, and sheer anguish. T.S. Eliot summarized the modern sense of time in precisely this way: in one of the *Quartets*, he say that, in this "drifting wreckage," it appears that

> ... the way up is the way down, the way forward is the way back.
> You cannot face it steadily, but this thing is sure. That time is no healer.

"Time surely would scatter all," says James Joyce's *Ulysses*; and the young hero of that novel remarks at a certain point: "History is a nightmare from which I am trying to awake." Which brings to a nice point the sort of baffled anguish that is everywhere so much a part of the sensibility that is expressed in the most representative literature of the past fifty or seventy-five years, when it confronts man's life in time.

So the whole question of death (as Amos Wilder has remarked) has, in effect, been relocated by the kind of imagination that controls the literature of our period. For the confrontation with nothingness does not any longer wait upon the moment of the actual death of the psycho-physical organism: on the contrary, meaninglessness and vacancy and the threat of non-being are felt as realities that require to be dealt with here and now. In short, "men are learning again that in the midst of life we are in death," [2] and it is from the angle of this perception that the literature of our time tends to explore the meaning of death.

Let me cite as an example the novel written by Albert Camus in

---

[2] Amos N. Wilder, "Mortality and Contemporary Literature", in: *The Modern Vision of Death*, ed. by Nathan A. Scott, Jr. (Richmond: John Knox Press, 1967), p. 23.

the early 1940's, the book which is entitled *The Stranger*. In the very narrative procedures that were here guiding Camus' art we can sense the essential thrust of the testimony being made, for it is the basic *form* of the novel which confirms what it most wants to convey, that to know the kind of abandonment which is man's ultimate fate is already to know the essential meaning of death. The narrative perspective is that of the central personage, Meursault: yet he appears quite incapable of the kind of ordering or evaluation of experience that the history of fiction has taught us to expect from the first-person narrator: indeed, the novel begins on a note of utter confusion:

> Mother died today. Or, maybe, yesterday: I can not be sure. The telegram from the Home says: YOUR MOTHER PASSED AWAY. FUNERAL TOMORROW. DEEP SYMPATHY. Which leaves the matter doubtful; it could have been yesterday.

And the protagonist's uncertainty about the exact time of his mother's death is of a piece with the confusion of mind that generally define his presence in the novel. His perceptions are disjointed because he inhabits a world that is out of joint and in which a man cannot easily take possession of his life. Always, he feels a "slow, persistent breeze" blowing in upon his life from "the dark horizon of [his] future", and it is this "slow, persistent breeze" that has a great levelling effect on his world, giving an equal significance to all actions and all experiences. When a neighbor offers him friendship, when a girl offers him her love, when his employer offers him the chance for advancement, when a priest offers him the comforts and consolations of religious faith, his unvarying response is either indifferent acceptance or indifferent refusal, for nothing makes much difference, given "the cruel mathematics that command our condition". Things have fallen apart, the center no longer holds — as Yeats says, "mere anarchy is loosed upon the world". So this man is a "stranger", an "outsider": he faces the world with a stubborn taciturnity because the world itself is silent: it is a gritty and mute, abandoned place without any thresholds at all, for here one does not live "on the borderland of something more." [3] Time has no threshold, for the immediately experienced moment is all that Camus' man has. Nor is he given a threshold by his relations with other persons, for he and they do not in any deep way interpenetrate one another. And, of course, the threshold of the Holy, the sense of living on the borderland between Nature and Supernature, between Time and Eternity — this is a threshold that is irretrievably and utterly gone.

It is, in other words — the universe inhabited by this man — a world that is absolutely profane. And it is, therefore, a world that is banal, that is mediocre, that is answerable to no principle of meaning at all. So the man whom we meet in Camus' novel is a creature ousted from the precincts of Grace, one something like those doomed ghosts in the pictures of the contemporary English painter Francis Bacon, who look out at the world heart-stricken and aghast. In short, the "death" of God appears to have brought nothing but death to the human spirit itself.

Now it is this general range of meaning that is being brought into view when modern literature is spoken of as having tended to relocate the whole issue of death. It is true, of course, that from Tolstoy's *Death of Ivan Ilych* to Hemingway's *Across the River and into the Trees* the literary imagination has regularly meditated on the brevity and transiency of human life, on the fact that we are "unreturning travellers" [4] who sit "at . . . sunset round a tomb". [5] But, even more regularly, the modern imagination has learnt to dwell on the many deaths that we die in the midst of life, and it is into this new dimension of things that the literature of

---

[3] Philip Wheelwright, *The Burning Fountain: A Study in the Language of Symbolism* (Bloomington: Indiana University Press, 1954), p. 8.

[4] John Hall Wheelock, "Silence", in: *A Little Treasury of Modern Poetry*, ed. by Oscar Williams (New York: Charles Scribner's Sons, 1946), p. 138.

[5] Mark Van Doren, "This Amber Sunstream", in: *A Little Treasury of Modern Poetry*, ed. by Oscar Williams, p. 143.

our period is prone to take the old problem of human mortality. What is most often lamented is not the fact that there comes a time when our breathing comes to an end — but, rather, it is loss of meaning, it is loss of faith, it is our loss of one another, it is these things that are lamented in such representative modern texts as Dostoievski's *The Possessed* and Conrad's *Heart of Darkness* and Eliot's *Waste Land* and Ford Madox Ford's *The Good Soldier* and Malcolm Lowry's *Under the Volcano* and Beckett's *Waiting for Godot*. And it is in terms of these characteristic losses of modern men that the problem of death has, I think, generally been explored in the literature of our age.

Now I should like to suggest in conclusion that this relocation of the problem of death from the dimension of Eternity to the dimension of Time is a development which may to some extent render the modern imagination ultimately more open to what is the real heart of the Christian hope for man's destiny. And, as we were reminded a few years ago by the English theologian John Robinson, the real heart of the Christian hope is perhaps nowhere expressed more succinctly in the New Testament than in the twentieth and twenty-first verses of the Epistle to the Philippians, where we are told: "Our commonwealth is in heaven, and from it we await a Saviour, the Lord Jesus Christ, who will change our lowly body to be like his glorious body, by the power which enables him even to subject all things to himself." And Dr. Robinson asks us to notice that this text is, in the first place, telling the Christian man that his commonwealth or citizenship is in heaven. "Whatever else that means," says he,

> . . . it means that heaven is where we already belong. "Passports for heaven" is a phrase which sums up one whole way of thinking about Christianity. But if the Christian holds a passport, it is not a passport to get him to heaven [after death], but a passport from heaven to live within this world as the representative and ambassador of a foreign style of life. In Moffatt's inspired rendering, the Church's function is to be a colony of heaven —

because its members are already by baptism citizens of heaven. [6]

In other words,

> ... the Christian hope is not so much a hope for heaven as a hope *from* heaven: for "from it we await a Saviour, the Lord Jesus Christ." The heart of the Christian hope is not that the housing committee of the celestial city council will one day move us from this slum to that "other country" ... The heart of the Christian hope is rather that the life of God ... will so penetrate the life of man ... that God's will shall be done on earth as it is in heaven. [7]

In short, the gospel of the reign of God is wrongly understood, if it is taken to mean that the world is simply "a vast transit camp, in which the Church's job is to issue tickets for heaven and pack people off to paradise": [8] it is, rather, a gospel which speaks about "the redemption of the body" — "that is, the reintegration of the whole man in all his relationships ... in a new solidarity which creates personality rather than destroys it." [9] And this is a gospel which declares that into that structure of life of which the Church is a kind of earnest the whole of life will ultimately be transformed, "by the power which enables him even to subject all things to himself." In other words, the gaze of the Christian man, as Dr. Robinson says, "is not at death, nor even beyond it at the skies, but at God's world," [10] and his concern is properly with his responsibility to join with Christ in ministering to the broken and the bruised, the insulted and the rejected, the despairing and the

---

[6] John A.T. Robinson, *On Being the Church in the World* (Philadelphia: Westminster Press, 1960), pp. 132–133.
[7] *Ibid.*, p. 133.
[8] *Ibid.*
[9] *Ibid.*
[10] *Ibid.*, p. 134.

needy. Which is to say that the goal of the Christian man is not some celestial city but that new world-order "of which within this world he is the ambassador and the agent." [11]

And what I'm wanting in conclusion to suggest is that this authentically realist note of the New Testament is something which, for all of its negativism, much of the characteristic literature of our period may to some extent help us to recover, in so far as it encourages us to relocate the issue of death from the dimension of the End of the dimension of the Here and the Now. Indeed, I suspect that, despite its frequently radical secularity, the literary imagination of our age may prove in all sorts of surprising ways to be a kind of *preparatio* for a deep recovery of what is at the heart of the Christian message. For, in relocating the ultimate problem of human existence from the dimension of Eternity to the dimension of time, it puts us in touch with a sense of reality that ought to be thought of as deeply a part of the authentically Christian vision of man's life in the world.

[11] *Ibid.*

Alexander COMFORT

Changing the life span

DR. ALEXANDER COMFORT was born in England in 1920. The wide range of interests included in his career are reflected in his educational background which combined the classics and the sciences.

He was both the Robert Styring Scholar in Classics and Senior Scholar in Natural Sciences at Trinity College, Cambridge University, where he received his undergraduate degree.

He has established two outstanding careers as an author and as a scientist. In the field of literature he is a poet, novelist, playwright and critic. Two of his novels, *The Power House* (1944) and *On This Side of Nothing* (1949) have received critical acclaim. He has been a tireless worker in pacifist causes. He refused military service in World War II and for a time was blacklisted as a broadcaster as a result of his bitter attacks upon the policies of the Western Powers, particularly the adoption of indiscriminate bombing.

His interests in the science field range over a wide spectrum. In recent years he has become one of Europe's acknowledged experts in the aging process. In 1967 he was president of the British Society for Research on Aging.

There are two experiences with which mankind has very great difficulty in coming to terms, even temporarily. One of these is death, the end of identity. Human beings have, as we know, a fixed life span, the fixity of which, I think, is perhaps more clearly seen if we put it in days. We have a life span of about 28 000 days. There is a date, in other words, on which I can predict with considerable confidence that, however careful, however heroic, or however lucky I may be, I shall no longer be alive. This is a familiar enough idea and we deal with the prospect by postponing it into the future. We shall certainly die, but fortunately not just yet. If we set a more definite date to the occurrence, our defenses tend to crumble. That is probably why cancer, which is by no means the most terrible terminal illness, has come to inspire such awe. We know the length of the fuse. It rather resembles that unpleasant skeleton in medieval dances of death which waltzes through the room tapping the dancers on the shoulder.

I am not, however, going to dwell on death. Before the day of our death, there is another date, perhaps fifteen years earlier, when we shall be alive, but not fully. Unlike disease, which if we are lucky and if we don't smoke too many cigarettes and or eat too much we may hope to escape, aging is one condition from which we are all going to suffer. Aging is impairment; it is the progressive dissolution of what we have built up throughout our lives, what William Yeats calls

"... the death
of every brilliant eye
that made a catch in the breath".

We deal with that one by thinking about something else or by talking about the compensations of age. One doesn't ask for compensation, in my submission, unless one has been run over. Few of the compensations of age survive an open-eyed visit to an old folks' home. And I must say that as a physician who became interested in this subject when I came in contact with geriatric medicine during the War, I have no patience with those who philosophize about the beauty of a green old age. I've seen too much of it occupationally. Aging is loss; it is not ripening. One goes around the wards and one realizes that these women were once beautiful, or at least young; these men were once people, and we no longer treat them as people. The only thing which has inhibited us from admitting to ourselves the enormity of this thing which is going to happen to us is that so far its course and its timing have seemed inevitable. If it is really inevitable, then presumably we'd better accept it with dignity. But all the evidence suggests that time-wise it is probably not inevitable, and this is the first generation in which, if we wish it and if we apply ourselves, we can say we have a fighting chance of seeing the onset of this intolerable and personally diminishing change rolled back. That possibility is a great deal nearer than most people realize, and that is why I want to address myself to it.

I think it is of great importance that those of us who work in a field of this kind should, as it were, give advance notice to the people who will have to cope with the situation which is in prospect of the sort of time scale which we have in mind.

Science may affect human longevity favorably in two quite distinct ways: it may suppress causes of premature death, or it may postpone the aging process which causes our liability to disease and death to increase logarithmically with the passing of time. The first of those two operations, which involves suppressing causes of premature death, has been highly successful. It has already meant that in the privileged countries more and more people reach the so-called "specific age" (75–80 years), but it hasn't altered that age appreciably. In fact, there is no evidence that it has changed since the time of Moses and Pharaoh. Throughout human history people have died before they reached old age, but if they reached the age of 70 they became old; if they reached the age of 80 they became older still. The second, and quite distinct operation, which is now in the stage of active research, is aimed at finding out why aging occurs and whether and, if so, how it can be slowed down by a fundamental interference with the clock mechanism.

I think it is important to recognize the very big difference between this approach, which is based on the search for a systems breakthrough, and the sum of all the rest of socio-medical advances. The curve of survival has gradually been pushed out until it has got squarer and squarer. but the ends of it remain pegged. The large changes in that curve represent quite simply the removal of causes of premature death, but the age at which we become old, judged by the criteria of growing infirmity and growing liability to die, and number of disease processes present, has undergone very little change throughout history.

Nobody dies of old age. Well, that is probably strictly true, but if you perform a post mortem upon a man of forty, the average number of potential causes of death present is one. If you perform a post mortem on a man of eighty, the average number of potential causes of death present approaches nine. Aging tends to represent an increase in the number and diversity of things which are wrong with us.

In the sense that the gerontologists use it, of course, aging is a process resulting in increased instability, failure of homeostasis. This loss of information is multiform, but its rate is very stable. Every species has a pretty sharp specific age and this stability is the basis of the well-justified assurance of actuaries — the people who work out our pensions and our insurance policies — that all premature causes of death apart, an annuitant is likely to die between the age of 70 and 100, regardless of any advance in the cure or prevention of specific diseases. You can kill yourself a lot sooner, but you can't make yourself go much longer. There is a biological limit on human longevity, a sort of wall, if you like, which is represented by the condition in which nobody dies at all before the age of 60 and everybody must still be dead by the age of about 105. And we're not going to make any difference to this by conventional improvements in medicine or in living conditions. Advanced societies are just about pushing the practical limits of public health in prolonging life. Most of the disease which is now seen by office physicians which is not psychosomatic is probably degenerative. The expectation of life at birth has, of course, increased steadily over the last century, but the expectation at 65 years has changed little or at all; it's risen by 2 years since 1901.

There is this ideal curve in which, as I say, nobody would die except by accident before the age of 60 or 70 and everybody is dead by the age of 100. And there is a law of diminishing returns. You can do the sums, and it has been computed by Robert Kohn at Western Reserve that if we were able totally to cure or abolish the three leading causes of natural death in the United States, which are cardiovascular disease, cerebrovascular disease and tumors in variety, this would be great for people who get those things when they are young; it would lead to an overall increase in the expectation of life of 7 years. But all of that would be represented by the cure of people who have these things young, and the increase in the expectation of life at age 65 would be a mere 2.5 years. The same is going to apply to all piecemeal therapeutic, supportive, medical, social, political measures. The patching up of single age-dependent conditions is frightfully costly, it's of limited usefulness in increasing the quality of life, it raises a lot of more unpleasant issues of medical priority and of hogging of facilities by privileged people and, all in all, it has very little further to give us in extending the period of adult vigor.

Biological interference with the actual rate of aging, however, is quite a different kettle of fish. It would move the curve over to the right and it's ready for test in man now, as soon as aging rates can be made measurable in the individual in the short term; I think it is virtually certain that such experiments will be started within the next decade and possibly sooner.

Now, we can increase the active life span of rats and mice by between 10 and 40 per cent. We can do it, and this is important, by relatively simple and unheroic manipulations. I'll come to some of those subsequently.

The reason that human experiments on this haven't been done long ago has nothing to do with ethics. It is quite simply that, if I give you a pill which is going to make you live to be a hundred, it is going to take upwards of 70 years to see whether it has worked; and in consequence experiments on people have been out by reason of tedium. One can work only on rats and mice just so long as one has to conduct the old-style, classical experiment of giving diet, exercise, treatment, what have you, to one group and not to another and seeing which group lives longer. Similar work in man is an impractical project which no body will fund and no pharmaceutical firm is willing to embark on. But we can now get over this and, in fact, the technique of overcoming it is one of the very few beneficial spin-offs from the atom bomb. It was developed originally to measure whether the survivors of Hiroshima were aging faster than usual as the result of radiation exposure. It was developed at Brookhaven by the Atomic Bomb Casualty Commission. The technique is very simple. A lot of things change with age; we know that our hair grays, our muscles weaken, our skin gets less elastic, our chemistry changes, our psychometric tests change. With a computer we make a battery inventory of all these things which change with age. We can then test a treated and untreated population. It should be feasible to demonstrate agents which are capable of causing all those parameters to change less rapidly in a treated group, and we are on the verge of being able to do this. I am now stumping the country to try to get somebody to fund this, because it is a bigger project than any one investigator can take on. It's bound to happen in the near future and we are now engaged in working out exactly what goes in the battery. Clearly they have to be things people will hold still for. You can measure grip capacity and you can measure skin elasticity, but if they are going to have to swallow stomach tubes or have thrice weekly testicular biopsies or something of this kind, you are going to lose your subjects before very long. We can do it, however, and we can do it with simple tests.

The type of experiment which is in mind would be to take a group of males, age 50, say, 200 in each group — males because we want to avoid the menopausal discontinuity — males at 50 because this is an age when most of the parameters will change significantly over two to three years. We could then run a two to three year experiment. We would see, first of all, whether the man who is aging fast on his skin is also aging fast on his psychometric tests. We would compare and pick out the extremes and correlate them. We would be able to see if there were any genetic or environmental groups identifiable who were aging faster or slower than usual. At the moment we have no way of knowing whether environmental factors affect the rate of aging. If corn flakes make you age faster or slower, the only way we could find this out would be retrospectively. The type of study I had in mind might reveal quite a lot of interesting things on these lines. We would also then be able to compare a group who'd been treated with a group who have not.

The manipulations which one has in mind are those which have been used in rats and in mice and they are really quite various. I'm not going to go into the science of this in great detail. But the chief manipulations which are up for tests at the moment are first of all calorie restriction. If you feed rats or mice 60 per cent of their ad libitum calorie intake you greatly prolong their life, and you postpone aging; all in all, you make them stay apparently much younger for very much longer, and this without retarding their growth seriously. This has been known since the 30's. The second, is the administration of antioxidants. If you read the small print on your packet of peanuts you will see that they contain permitted antioxidants. Antioxidants are things that are put into food and into man-made materials such as rubber to protect the molecules from chemical attack. Now, Denham Harman in Omaha had the bright idea that these agents might protect the ingredients of the body against long-term chemical attack. He tested them and he found that mice which were treated with food antioxidants lived longer. Before we give three cheers for antioxidants, one must remember, however, that we are giving 0.5 per cent of the diet, which is an immense quantity of antioxidant, and we may merely be spoiling the mouse's appetite by making him eat a large amount of a nauseous chemical, so this may be a repetition of the dietary effect. Secondly, not all of them work. Those which work are the antioxidants which are powerful liver enzyme inducers. I hate to say it, but we are now testing DDT, phenobarbital and cyclamates, all of which on some evidence may prolong a mouse's life, to see whether by virtue of their enzyme inducing activity they are actually beneficial to longevity. Quite an interesting point when we talk about food additives.

Thirdly, there is the question of immunological manipulation. With the passage of time the body's defenses against both bacteria and mis-specified body cells appear to change. You can argue whether the crooks become more virulent or whether the police of the body are getting older, or even whether the police go wrong and arrest innocent cells and innocent citizens, but there is a large battery of experimentation which is now being carried out, and which is very important because one special case of cell mis-specification is cancer. The majority of cancer cells which appear in the body we appear to get rid of by ourselves and it's possible that in learning to control aging we should get a great deal better idea of immunological methods of attacking cancer. Anyway, those are some of the things, and there are quite a number of other techniques, which I won't elaborate on here, by which it is possible to interfere with the rodent life span. I have put them in the order of immediate applicability because the most obvious one to try in humans is diet. That is one where we should run into no trouble with the FDA, and where we could go ahead tomorrow.

After all, cutting down the calories in a person's diet is not a very great hardship and the sort of experiment we have in mind would be no bigger and no more arduous than those that are now going on to see whether margarine is better for heart disease than butter.

Supposing we were to succeed in transferring rodent techniques to man and supposing we were able to do it straightaway, the result hopefully would be that a treated man of 80 (if we assume a 10-year gain) would have the same health and the same disabilities that he would have had at 70. Now, we all know that there is a big scatter in the manifestations of aging. Bertrand Russell or Artur Rubinstein are fit in their 80's; another man may be very old for his age. To make a 10-year difference would not immediately be very evident; it would probably only mean that more of us were like Artur Rubinstein and fewer of us were like the old man who is bedridden. The prediction based on rodent work and on the work which has been done on radiation life shortening is that, by affecting the rate of aging, most, and quite possibly all, of the changes in a given individual would be postponed roughly in step, across the board; everything from tumors to pedestrian road accidents, which are highly age-correlated, would occur at later ages. There may be some processes that would be resistant to this, there may be some non-aging processes such as growth of the eye lens which would give rise to trouble if people lived long enough. We just don't know this. But, in general, we reckon that there is a good chance of postponing, as in rats and mice, all of the aging causes, all of the causes of death, roughly in step. What is important to realize is that the period of senility would not be prolonged; in other words, you would become old later, you would not be old for longer.

The argument for investment in experimental gerontology and the search for this sort of systems breakthrough depends on some facts which we can catalog. First of all, there is no other way of getting longer, vigorous life; secondly, it looks as if it could be done; thirdly, it ought to be easier to affect a rate than to rewrite a program. In other words, it ought to be easier to make cancer or high blood pressure happen later than to cure them when they happen or to stop them happening at all. Other specific medical research directed to single diseases is obviously necessary, but it would find many of its tasks subsumed in any general understanding of the aging process because so many of these conditions are, in fact, partially degenerative.

Now, the last point that I make there is that it is extremely likely that an empirical way of slowing human aging will anticipate our knowing how aging works. We are much more likely to find things which will alter the human life span before we find out exactly how they work. When Hahn and Strassmann discovered uranium fission they, without knowing it, opened the door to practical fission energy, and technological forecasters refer to what they call the Hahn–Strassmann point; that is, the point in an investigation when it becomes clear that something is feasible and is worth looking at from the point of view of application. That point has, I think, now passed almost unnoticed in gerontology. We are now in line to get on with this. Not only that, but forecasting is possible. We can first of all predict that direct experiment on delaying age changes in man is, from what I have seen around the country, virtually certain to be in hand by 1975; probably at more than one center. The second thing we can say is that if the techniques we use in rodents work in man, or if we're lucky, then allowing for most of the normal research delays — you'll notice in technological forecasting we always overestimate the progress over five to ten years and underestimate the progress in fifteen to twenty years — then the probability is that some agent demonstrably reducing the rate of mature human aging is likely to be known within fifteen years. The possible amount of the increase could be anything from 0 to 100 per cent, but I think on the rodent analogy the likelihood would be that it would be in the range of 10 to 20 per cent increase in vigorous life. You can't predict the limits, and of course with every new gain we got there would be a staircase effect: it would give us more time for research. That represents the lower limit of speed in development, given the present investment which isn't very big — it's about 7.5 million dollars annually for this country which is the biggest spender on it.

Now, if the rat and mouse type procedures don't work on human aging when they are started late in human life of if we find that the postponement of the age changes is partial or unequal or has got side effects, the future rate of progress is going to depend roughly on how much funding we get. But I think once the machinery and the experience for direct human experimentation have been created, we can expect a pretty rapid application, and the creation of this machinery for use with harmless procedures is the next priority for research planning.

The technical approaches to age control are various and they depend on the hypotheses of aging, none of which are now confirmed. Most of these contain the idea that age damage is a process of information loss through increasing chemical error. It is probably located in the sequence DNA—RNA—sythetases—proteins. To cut through all this and not dwell on chemistry, if aging is a process of noise accumulation, that's one thing; if it's a process of running out of program, that is something else. If we had a phonograph record which scratches every time we play it, ultimately it will become unplayable and we can slow that loss of information down by lubricating the needle and keeping out the dust. If we have one of those records they used to circulate to advertise language schools, which was on a postcard, and you could only play it once, but not restart it, then we might make the performance last longer, but we can only do it by running it more slowly, though not so much more slowly as to spoil the music. The main predictive point is that if we get an empirical effect on the rate of aging in man, we do not need to find out exactly what we're doing. We'll more than likely find out the nature of the aging process by seeing what modifies it. That may sound an unscientific view, but it happens pretty often in medicine. The Wassermann reaction for syphilis, which was a keystone of preventive medicine, was developed on an entirely erroneous assumption, but it still worked; we still use it. Now, all in all, I think we can assume that by the year 1990 we may well know of an experimentally efficacious way of prolonging vigorous life by 20 per cent. Of course, we shall have to wait for the subjects to live on into age to be sure, but we should have an inferential ground for thinking that we have that by 1990. You have to remember always the built-in lag due to the human life span. The second point is that the agents are likely to be simple and cheap; they won't depend on intensive care units, large physical apparatus, or transplants of major organs, and that solves a lot of problems. I think that the direct application will be possible at about the same rate as antibiotics have been applied worldwide, and I think that all existing medical services and governments will at least elect to apply them, or if not that, be unable to prevent their application, rather as with The Pill. So, I think we had better get used to the idea. My only reservation on application is for the case where longevity depended on very long and tiresome dietary restriction. The model of cigarette smoking shows that the public is not willing, out of concern for longevity, to make itself uncomfortable. In that case we would wait until my pharmaceutical friends have developed what they call the "pig pill", which would enable you to eat as many calories as you like without absorbing them — a rather disgusting idea to my mind reminiscent of the Emperor Caligula. In case you think I'm playing this off the top of my head, the predictions I am giving you here are those of two Delphi studies of scientists, one done by Smith, Kline and French and the other by the Rand Corporation, which gave median dates of 2023 and 2017 for the years in which this thing would be in full operation.

The implication of success in modifying the rate of aging needs to be based on this sort of model: perhaps a 15 to 20 per cent increase, and not on the 200—300 year life spans which some futurologists have talked about. They're just possible, but they aren't terribly likely. But we've got to do a lot of thinking. The things we have to think about are demographic, economic, political, psychological, philosophical. We've got to make a little examination of our current attitudes to aging in British and United States culture, because the United States is the society which is most likely to achieve the systems breakthrough. I have been around to examine what other countries are doing and this is very much where it's at.

Postponement of aging is unlikely to subsume, though it might eventually be arranged to give, the abolition of eventual senility. Aldous Huxley's model, where you have a generation who lived in apparent youth for 70 years and then snuffed out, is biologically pretty unlikely. It won't involve putting people into hibernation; it won't involve prolonging childhood; it won't involve any other fancy tricks. It will simply be a matter of slowing down a clock. But one of the important things to realize is that from the moment we get any change, all past actuarial experience, which is still on a very solid floor so far, goes right for six, and the actuaries are getting a bit worried about this. You remember the saint who walked when his head was cut off: the remark was made that it was the first step that counts, and this applies here. We've only got to make a half per cent change in the life span to make a very big shake-up in business prediction.

Demographically — now this is something that's in everybody's mind — longer life is going to involve an increase in population. We were so worried about it that we did a scenario for the computer. We made the assumption that by 1990 there would be two ways of prolonging human life by 15 per cent each and that the two were cumulative; in other words, if you had both, you got 30 per cent. And we said, let us say that one is simple and easy like taking a pill and the other is complicated, having an operation. We fed into the computer the rate at which penicillin and kidney grafts have spread world-wide and from that you could compute the probable change in the world's population from this cause alone.

By the year 2020 that scenario gives an increase of 7 per cent from this cause as against a doubling every 33 years from all other causes. So, we've got to control population anyway whether we control aging or not. There is a further important point to remember, and that is that in animals reproductive rate is inversely correlated with longevity. Long-lived animals are low reproducers. If we are going to aim at zero population growth, then we need long-lived people; the two fit together rather well. So, I think, the slogan is: Zero population growth and long-term people.

The gain we envisage is wholly in the productive, nondependent years. At present education is getting longer. Most people spend 30 per cent of their life span — no, the first 30 years, which is more than 30 per cent — becoming fully experienced, and then have about another 30 years of active life. After that they begin to dwindle. Our gain would be in the middle section. It wouldn't be very important in this country; it might even give rise to problems. How important it would be to subsistence economies, I don't really know. We have to, in any case, update our attitudes to the old; we already fail to use our older citizens — at any rate we do in Britain. The number of Americans now 65 or older is 16.6 million, and even without our interference, by 1990 that number will have increased to 27 million. What our research would mean would be that more of those people would be fit and more of them would be active in the community. The portion of the life span over which each citizen remains a potential contributor to the economy will depend in the 1990's and later upon education and retirement policy and not on the results of our research.

The financial results of a possible systems breakthrough, have been insufficiently realized; and I will not dwell on them here. Whether the gain on insurance from the non-decease of life policy holders would offset the losses from increased survival of annuitants, I leave it to the trade to work out; it's not my job.

The psychological and political and philosophical implications are obviously less easy to assess. Longer life means slower turn-

over, both of persons in office and of generations. The old style
Oriental used to say, "Oh, King live forever" but he said it in the
knowledge that the king wouldn't live forever and he was pretty
safe. Every personal tyranny has its term. More significant, of
course, is that with a slower turnover, the discrepancy between
learned attitudes and actuality which is now reflected in politics
and in the generation gap might be increased. I don't know how
far adaptability is inherent and therefore a biologically modifiable
character and how far it depends on social roles. A tenure of office
for administrators, executives and professors increased by 40 per
cent cannot be viewed with total complacency.

The psychological implications of a demonstrable breach in the
age barrier are even less calculable, but I am quite sure they are
important. We don't know what proportion of human unconscious
attitudes are determined by the awareness, not only of death, but
of death at a fixed time. I think a lot of our behaviors are geared
to our consciousness of the shape of the present human life cycle.
Psychoanalysts have done less on this than writers like Unamuno
in his "Tragic Sentiment of Life". A change which made the
human life cycle more open-ended could have, I think, very great
effects on our attitude; I wouldn't like to predict what those
would be.

There is one other psychological matter which I want to bring
to your attention and this has a bearing on research priorities.
Scientific research in modern societies, so far from being rationally
directed, has taken on, to an anthropologist at least, a lot of the
functions performed in primitive societies by magic. The logical
observer would be surprised to see how many of our respectably
purposive procedures are actually fueled by unconscious fantasy.
Travel to the moon is, I suppose, our most modern exploit, but it
also happens to be the prototypic exploit of the Eskimo wizard.
Indefinite prolongation of life is another of these exploits and for
that reason I think it may well get funded. The more like magic it
is, the more likely there is to be money for it. Normally, one can

only get funding on a vast scale in any society now, as one knows, if one puts up a destructive project or one which inflates the ego of somebody in office. These things appeal to institutional psychopaths but magical-type projects can run them very close and scientists who are concerned with serious projects, who want to bring about actual changes in society or carry out constructive things, have become shamelessly adept at making use of these responses to bamboozle public figures into supporting worthwhile projects against their will. I'll say no more about it, but I think that aging research will get funded. And it will, in fact, be one of the first.

It has an interesting philosophical implication in that if we do prolong life it's one of the first major instances I know in which science could be said to produce an artificial betterment of biological function. Normally, the doctor is trying to restore normality; here we would be trying to go one better than normality. More important, I think, again, is the possibility that there may be an anguished and unproductive theological argument between the naturalist view — that turnover is good in itself, it shouldn't be resisted by the individual out of a selfish desire to survive, and you mark my words, no good will come of it — and the general humanist position that the quintessence of respect for people is to keep them going as individuals so long as they are getting a life of a quality which justifies it. This argument has been obscured in the past by the fact that the attainable preservation wasn't very good. Fortunately for the humanist view, which you may gather I hold to be the right one, the initial systems breakthrough is likely to be passed before the argument becomes general, so that, as in the case with birth control, Hudibrastic arguments will come too late and the public will have voted with its feet.

I think there could even be a moral effect of greater longevity. The prospect of greater longevity now and further longevity later could enhance our respect for life, if only in terms of our respect for our own skin, in which we would have a bigger stake still. I think our respect for death, our own and other people's, has increased quite markedly with the decline in the conviction of spiritual immortality. But in present-day developed societies the old are in a pretty bad posture. To a humane individual who has had the opportunity to observe aging in depth, not in selected vigorous individuals, and particularly in our own society which notably mistreats the old, the existence of old age is simply not tolerable. The biological losses which go with age are undergone in all cultures, but the simpler societies often do provide real compensations. To the biological losses of aging our culture adds loss of role, loss of activity, loss of self-esteem, and loss of social worth. Old people have to contend with natural senescence, with the effects of inflation, with the pressures of socioanthropological attitudes to dependence, to modernity and to achievement, (achievement for us is always prospective; past achievement doesn't score) and also a whole battery of unconscious fears, which tend to manifest themselves as active dislike on the part of the young and the physician. It's a curious thing that the old in many societies are now coming to be another kind of underprivileged minority, and it's a rather remarkable comparison. We talk now of Black Power. If there were as many rich and powerful and decision-taking Black people in this society as there are rich, powerful and decision-taking old people, Black Power would have been a reality, and I wonder why it is that Old Power isn't a reality. I wonder why, in other words, our society allows the old, who are well-represented in administration, to be another under-privileged group. That's true here and is certainly true in Britain. And this is curious because it is a group we shall all join. One can be born poor, or one can be born an immigrant, and then one may transcend it, but we shall all *become* old. I think that this is one of the more curious political manifestations of our time, but I think it will have some repercussions in the next few years.

I have mentioned that, not because I am going to talk about old age, but because it has sharpened our sense of the intolerability of aging at a time when we are in a posture to do something about it.

Obviously, we are not going to *abolish* old age; we will still age, but we shall age later; we shall still encounter all of these problems, but we shall encounter them later; and our work may have the effect of a catalyst, and lead to the attitude that old age having been seen to be intolerable, our culture must also see if it is preventable or at least postponable. This is quite a real effect; it's very much the attitude taken up by Alan Harrington in his book *The Immortalists* and I think that the shift of expectation he describes, and of dissatisfaction with our present lifespan, is important.

The reversibility of existing age changes is perhaps something that I should deal with before I conclude. We have arrived at the point at which the present human life span is unacceptable, just as the infant and the maternal mortalities of a hundred years ago were unacceptable. We can look forward to a slowing of aging in the near future and we can look beyond that to a rather longer term future. The reversibility of age changes is very difficult to forecast, and I think at all events it is less likely to be wholesale in its effect on aging and is very much further away in time. If the information loss with aging is molecular and if it affects the primary molecular copies in the DNA, then there's not much chance, I think, of reversing it once it's happened. If it occurred further down the chain, as Leslie Orgel has proposed, in the translation to synthetases, then there is at least in theory the possibility of scrubbing the faulty synthetases and having recourse to the original copies. But nobody has yet found a way of growing new hair on bald men, de-wrinkling old skin or unfurring old arteries and I think it will be a very long time before we can do that. We will concentrate our attention accordingly on the slowing down of the aging process.

Now, let me, just to finish, and at the risk of tedium, reiterate exactly what it is we are and we are not trying to do. We are trying to tamper with the taxi meter so you are going to get more miles for your dollar. We are trying to alter the clock so that it takes eighty years to get to be sixty. We are not trying to prolong infirm old age; if we were to find that we were prolonging life without prolonging the quality of life, without prolonging adult vigor, we should have failed and we should have to go back to square one. We are not trying to spin out childhood, though that, too, is probably feasible. We shall aim initially to start any experimental procedure around the age of 40 to 50, simply to reduce the duration of the procedure. If it won't work that late in life, we shall have to move to an earlier age group until we find one in which it does. From the rat work you can't predict, accordingly, how many of those here present will be in a posture to benefit if they wish from any successes we may have. The methods which are used are likely to be simple and cheap. This is very fortunate because I would have very grave doubts about the whole thing if they weren't going to be. They would otherwise involve grave problems of priority, of hogging by the rich, of hogging by political bosses, etc. From our present information those problems are not very likely to arise, and we should be able to see that no power group can hog these benefits or keep them secret or prevent their use, which at least is a cheering thought.

I am as opposed as anyone is to the idiot abuse of technology, but the effects which are likely to arise from altering the human life span, though they're not all of them problem-free, don't keep me awake at night. We have done our homework, I assure you, on these effects. I think if we succeed it will be a great and a worthy victory for man. What worries me most about it is that so few people outside the immediate subject, scientists included, realize just how close this breakthrough might be. America, as I say, is the country where on present form it is going to happen. To my mind, as a foreigner, it makes a very good American project: it has the sort of humane, practical empiricism which I think Ben Franklin and his friends would have approved of. It belongs to a very good tradition, as we see it, that if human life is nasty, brutish and short we should quit talking edifying philosophy about it and start the attempt to see if something can't be done about it practically. I think Ben Franklin would have approved that view.

Now, if it happens, most of you here are going at least to see it happen and you're going to have to handle it. It could be as big a revolution in terms of medicine as the control of infectious disease and it could be a much more far-reaching revolution in its social and psychological scope. I say, don't let's be scared of it; it's one of the advances which is brewing in biology which we don't need to be scared of; and let's get on with it. It's a development in human control of human destiny and that seems to be a good thing. It seems that it should restore a little of the confidence we've lost. And we need to regain that confidence, which has a lot to do with our awareness of death and our feeling of the shape of life, I think. Perhaps the rational anger and the militancy which go with confidence is something we might recover to make the extra years worth living. The various interests who through negligence and self-interest and psychopathology cheat people out of life will in the future be cheating them out of something which is even more precious than it is today, and I would like to hope that the new potential which comes from longer, vigorous life could be the last straw to break our toleration of that deception, but then, like the rest of us on this platform, in very different ways, I am a revolutionist as well as a biologist.

Krister STENDAHL

Immortality is too much and too little

DR. KRISTER STENDAHL was born in Stockholm in 1921. Following his formal education he was ordained a priest of the Church of Sweden in 1944.

After that followed graduate work at Cambridge, England, and in Paris as well as Uppsala University where he received the Doctor of Theology degree in 1954. During this ten-year period he also served two years as a pastor in the diocese of Stockholm and two years as chaplain at Uppsala University.

He joined the Harvard Divinity School faculty in 1954 and became John H. Morison Professor of New Testament Studies in 1958. From 1963 to 1968 he was Frothingham Professor of Biblical Studies. In 1968 he was appointed Dean of the Divinity School and became John Lord O'Brian Professor of Divinity.

In addition to serving as editor of the Harvard Theological Review, Dean Stendahl does extensive writing in Swedish, German and American Journals and encyclopedias including *The Gospel of Matthew* in Peakes Commentary (1962) and the essay on Biblical Theology in *The Interpreter's Dictionary of the Bible* (1962). He is the editor and co-author of *The Scrolls and the New Testament* (1957). He is a Fellow of the American Academy of Arts and Sciences.

Dr. Stendahl preferred to let his address retain the style of oral presentation in which it was delivered at the conference.

Religious man in his faith, in his speaking and singing about God, is actually seeking — and seeking to express — his place in the total universe. He is trying to cope with reality. And religious men and women through the ages have done that within the knowledge of their time, within the science of their time, as well as within other insights and wisdom. The conflict between science and religion has, if I understand it right, never been a conflict between science and religion. It has been an unfortunate mistiming or comparing not equal to equal: when religious sanction was given to scientific insights of an earlier time, it often clashed with newer insights in the sciences. Thus the famous clashes between religion and science — theology and science — have usually been clashes between *sciences*. And yet the Church has lived through many serious transitions as to world views and scientific insights, and so have other religious communities. There was one such transition in the time of the early church fathers: the change from the three-story universe to the Ptolemaic view of the world. And then there was the Copernican one. And there is a slogan in my homeland which says that in the first generation the Church fights new scientific insights; in the second generation we say that those scientific views are adiaphora, i.e., they don't really make a difference to the essence of the faith, and in the third we write hymns on the basis of the new scientific insight. You all know that 19th century evening hymn which begins "The day thou gavest, Lord, is ended..." In it we sing: "The sun that bids us rest is waking, Our brethren neath the western sky. And hour by hour fresh lips are making, Thy wondrous doings heard on high". It is a beautiful Copernican hymn.

Now, there has always been, as that dialogue has gone on, a

certain tendency of plucking the flowers from the latest scientific insights, and we had a wonderful flower coming up before us here in George Wald's presentation. When he said that actually the entrance of death into this long chain of development coincided with the sexual mode of procreation, which is exactly what it says in Genesis 3, where the awareness of sexuality is combined with the entrance of death into the earlier paradise. But that's exactly the kind of examples preachers should not use glibly for it really is two different modes of speaking. A facile mixing of the language of science and the language of the Bible easily gives the believer the feeling that "Science proves the Bible", as if the Bible could not speak for itself in its own language.

I happen to believe that the whole long and glorious Christian tradition of speaking about the immortality of the soul, is only a period of the Judeo-Christian tradition, and that period may now be coming to an end. I am saying that with some trepidation and my trepidation is not for any other reason than that it is always painful to tear into what is very dear to many. And yet there come times in the history of theology and of the Christian community and the Church in which such changes take place. I have always loved the example of the Apostle Paul who understood what theologians have great difficulties in understanding: that sometimes there are new problems and new data. It is very hard for a theologian really to have respect for 'new data'. Partly he is in tune with the historians who always play the trick on us by showing that new data are really just little new twists of the old ones. Having so many old data as the historian has, (a) it's easy for him, and (b) he should have some reward for knowing so many data. So he has a tendency always of minimizing the new. But tradition, unless it is just museum tradition, living tradition is just as much a way of change as it is a means of continuity. You remember when Paul discusses matters of divorce and things like that in First Corinthians, chapter 7. He says, now there are certain cases of divorce and Jesus said that there should be no such and he quotes a word from the Lord. But then he says, "Now how is it then in special cases?" and he mentions certain special cases and Paul says, "On this one I have no word from the Lord." And I think he was the last preacher in Christendom who had the guts to admit that. But what is really involved in that is a respect for the new. He could just as well, could he not, have done what we all do: "Now, of course, we don't have exactly a word for that but it follows from what we have — bang, bang, bang..." That way one will always smother the newness.

The new insight, the new experience, is something to be taken seriously and I happen to believe that this should be our first observation when we think about immortality and the end of life in the perspective of the Christian tradition. Now, to outsiders this kind of speaking about new interpretations doesn't go over very well, because it always sounds as if: "Oh, those tricky theologians. Of course, they really have lost their faith but they have to somehow make something of it. So they are clever manipulators. Of course, they do not believe but after all they are earning their living on belief so they have to do something."

There is an attitude which I always have called "the fundamentalism of the non-believer" and that's the worst kind because it is one which takes for granted that "the Christian faith" or "the meaning of the Bible" is always the most sterile, unchangeable orthodoxy that could ever be imagined. That's at least honest, as they say. But as the rabbis already knew, there comes a moment, as they said, when there is time to do something for the Lord, and by that they meant a time for a new interpretation. Now, that's a little arrogant but it points in the right direction.

The question about immortality of the soul is interesting for someone who is primarily a Biblical scholar because he specializes in sixty-six so-called books that do not know of immortality of the soul. The word occurs in two places in the New Testament: once about God "who alone has immortality" (I Timothy 6:16), and once in a very special setting, where it is perhaps borrowed from other people whom Paul quotes when he speaks of how the mortal nature must put on immortality (I Corinthians 15:53ff.) But perhaps the almost complete absence of the word "immortality" is not really the point. The point is that the whole world which comes to us through the Bible, Old Testament and New, is not interested in the immortality of the soul. And if you think it is, it is because you have read it into the material. In terms of the Old Testament it is very clear that Abraham, Isaac and Jacob, and George Wald are one in believing that the only immortality that there is, is in the germ plasm, or they called it "the loins" (e.g., Genesis 35:11). The only immortality that the earlier strata of the Old Testament knows about is the perpetuation through your offspring. Theirs is a view of man created of dust who is made a human being by God's energizing power, the "spirit", being blown into the dust. That is also what Ecclesiastes speaks about in that beautiful description of aging, which outdoes T.S. Eliot because that's what he tried to copy, which ends on the note, as you know, that then, "the dust returns to earth, whence it came, and the spirit returns to God who gave it" (12:7). Here the spirit is not the individual's little identity spirit, but the life-giving power of God, the *ruach*, the wind which is withdrawn and so man disintegrates into dust. Dust to dust, ashes to ashes.

That's not much of immortality of the soul. And, the New Testament in a very interesting way speaks constantly about resurrection as against immortality. The interesting thing with this is not the discussion which has gone through the whole history of the Christian tradition of how resurrection relates to immortality and whether immortality is for the soul and resurrection is the way in which the body is added to that soul or whatever the relations between them are. That is a later question of theological speculation once the Christian message about the resurrection came up against the Hellenistic and secular pre-occupation with immortality. We should rather ask why and for what purpose the New Testament speaks about resurrection, why that is its proper way of speaking.

Learned scholars have found out — and that's not so hard to do — that the origins of this strange language of the resurrection are to be found in thoughts about martyrdom and that the question to which resurrection is the answer is not the question about what's going to happen to man when he dies. The question is not: What is going to happen to little me? Am I to survive with my identity or not? The question is rather whether God's justice will win out. The martyrs and the righteous are suppressed by the establishment — own or foreign — the rich are fat-eyed and happy and seem to carry the day while the righteous go down the drain. Resurrection answers the question of theodicy, i.e. the question of how God can win, the question of a moral universe. Does crime pay? Will evil win? Where is God's promise and power? Will God ultimately come through? Will the Kingdom come somehow so that righteousness flows forth and justice is in the midst of us all? That is the matrix, that is the womb out of which the dream and thought and hope and prayer for the resurrection emerged out of the Jewish community in times of martyrdom and suppression. They spoke about vindication of the righteous and the martyrs. They did not affirm so much the fate of such individuals. They were interested in whether God and Justice would have the last word.

You can see that in a strange way, if you are a careful Bible reader. There is a passage in Matthew (27:51-53), where on Good Friday itself, when Jesus dies and there is the earthquake (i.e., the cosmic forces join in the drama) the situation is so jittery, so to say, so that some of the righteous who had been suppressed were already coming out of their graves, and the general resurrection that one looked forward to, the ultimate establishment of justice in the world, was starting to happen.

So I'm just lecturing you on plain, descriptive Biblical studies. It's a simple fact that when Peter said to his friends up in Galilee, "You know, this Jesus whom they crucified and whom we loved so much is risen", the thoughts that went through these people's minds were not, "Oh, that means that there is eternal life for little me." That would be a rather odd way of making such a point. No, to them it meant that there was reason to believe that God's ultimate power of justice, vindicating the oppressed, the suppressed and the martyred, had manifested itself. Compare Acts 2:22-24, and the way in which Jesus had left his case in the hands of God the just vindicator (I Peter 2:23). The Kingdom had taken a big step forward as one had been praying, hoping and dreaming for its coming. So that the issue to which the most original Christian way of speaking about the end of life in the sign of the resurrection of Jesus was an issue that did not speak to the question of what is going to happen to my identity, but what is happening in and to the world. Is there reason to believe that justice will win out? It is a concern for where the world is going, not a concern for oneself.

I think about Easter sermons. There is, of course, the type of Easter sermon which capitalizes on the fact that it is spring and nature is coming back to life. It's beautiful, but I guess such preachers should be sent by their Mission Boards to the southern hemisphere for a couple of years. Or perhaps one should be more serious about it and say: No, if Easter means anything in the Christian tradition it rather means the breaking of the bonds of nature, in a certain sense, than the affirmation of the cycle of nature. And then, of course, there are those for whom primarily the meaning of Easter is the assurance as to eternal life and the immortality of the soul: the assurance as to the afterlife. And I don't know how it is with you or with people you know when the — what shall I call it — the role-play between congregations and pastors is broken through, and people say what they really think and are concerned about; but I think it is true to say that an increasing number of men and women are less and less concerned about the immortality of the soul, especially their own. That somehow it isn't that obviously attractive and commanding; the glow of the immortality language has worn off. And why has it, if that be true? It has so because that whole way of thinking and speaking which we, as I said, do not even have in the Bible is really part and parcel of a whole worldview which is basically built on a platonic view, a platonic philosophy, and a platonic understanding of reality — polarity between soul and body. And for centuries and centuries such a platonic model was not only maintained by the Church — and the Church never invented it — but it was the *lingua franca*, the common way of thinking about man and world. It seemed obvious and self-evident. But now on Easter day the Church in many cases has a double duty. First it has to convince man that he has that soul so that the message fits because there can be no joy unless he first has the need that the joy is supposed to satisfy. I happen to believe that that whole way of thinking, feeling and ultimately experiencing oneself in the world is on the way out.

On the other hand, this is not a sign of less human, existential, and ethical seriousness or religious seriousness on the side and part of modern man. What he is concerned about is not so much what is going to happen to him but what is going to happen to this poor world. He is just as concerned with the future of God's plan and creation, the future of justice: Is the Kingdom a dream or is it a dream worth believing in, a dream affirmed by God in Christ? That's what the problem is now to many, and as a biblical scholar I must note how that concern is in many ways similar to the concerns of the first Christians as they prayed for the coming of God's kingdom rather than for their own immortality.

And so I say that in that setting immortality and the concern for immortality appears much *too little*, too selfish, too preoccupied with myself or even my family, my race, my species. The question of prolonged identity somehow doesn't fit to what is really bothering us as we ask the questions of meaning and we seek the rays of hope. And immortality is *too much* since it has a tendency to claim to know more than may be good for us. It is too much because it is too specific, too tied up with a peculiar way of thinking about man, God, and the world. It is too much because it does not ring quite true to many a man's religious experience. Now, it's a funny thing that whenever something suggests itself to a person, even to a theologian, even to a preacher, and it isn't quite as it has always been, then he is always accused of being secular or something, being influenced from somewhere else. But it is in his religious experience and understanding that he finds that somehow this kind of language does not ring true. Against those who know too much, the first Epistle of John says:

> "Beloved, we are God's children now; it does not yet appear what we shall be, but we know that when he appears we shall be like him for we shall see him as he is".

The end of life is thus in the mystery of the will of God and in the coming of the Kingdom. The issue is not what happens to me but what happens to God's fight for His creation. What it is about is what we pray about in the Lord's Prayer which doesn't have a single word about little me. That's why it is such a great prayer and that's why it might even have come right straight from Jesus. Have you ever thought about that, that when you pray that prayer you really don't pray about yourself, but you just shout: Thy Kingdom come, Thy will be done, and you are just sort of swallowed up in the concern for the victory and the coming of the Kingdom? And that blows our minds out of preoccupation with ourselves. And it should. It opens up in our time a feeling for the fascination with the billions of years and the galaxies and the possibility of life on other planets (I have always hoped that there is something like it because it would put us in place, not to be so terribly preoccupied with our own importance).

The end of life is not in the question of or the concern for "my identity". And when I speak about the Kingdom and the victory of God and about Jesus then I say to myself: A life like his which was a kind of spearheading of the Kingdom coming into this world, a life like his was vindicated by God, was resurrected; a life in its weakness, in its death, with a power of weakness, the turning of the other cheek, all these strange things which I like to call the "operation headstart" for the Kingdom. I know, the world is just not ready yet for that life style; and we live in a nation that has no respect whatsoever for the power of weakness, or for that whole phenomenon of the coming of the Kingdom, of the Christians as the guinea pigs for the Kingdom, with what I term the eschatological "itch". You know, it is a very interesting thing that one has always thought about Jesus as teaching people patience and that is partly because of our way of speaking about and thinking about eternal life instead of thinking about the Kingdom. Religion has had a tendency of becoming, as Marx rightly said, an opiate for the people, handed out by those in the leading positions: of course, you can't have it all now but if you behave you will get it in the yonder somehow. It has given us an image of religion as serving toward patience. But when I read about my Jesus I know nothing less patient — less patient with evil, less patient with sickness, even less patient with death. He went to the attack, he pushed the coming of the Kingdom.

Now, what I am suggesting to you is that the proper image in the center of the Christian life as we look to the end of life is a new one, or rather an older one, one that should come back and engender new theology, new prayer, new faith, new bread and life — the image is the Kingdom, the coming of the Kingdom. That's what it is about. And that is why the whole concern for individual identity, which is the technical meaning of immortality of the soul, is not to be found in the Good Book because its concern and its focus is elsewhere.

Let me then just observe that in so doing, and especially in using and being inspired by the image of tenderness, love, and weakness in him who came, comes and will come with the Kingdom, we should perhaps also note that one of our problems at this time is not so much our powerlessness, but that we have in a way too much power. We can split the atom, we can manipulate the gene bank, we can make Einsteins galore, we can, we can, we can.... And we can certainly upset the balance of nature. George Wald has spoken already about the serious ways in which we must be prophets of doom and I guess both George Wald and I know that a true prophet is one who prays and hopes that he will be proven wrong. I think in a way that applies to Jesus. Jesus expected the end of the world in 40 years and the Bible-reading Christians ask, "Could Jesus be wrong?" But Jesus was a true prophet; he was one of those who prophesied as the Lord had told him and as he saw it but since he was a true prophet, his hottest dream was that his prophecy would not come true. And it didn't — but it looks pretty bad now.

Our problem is one of over-power and that's perhaps why we as human beings should take a lower posture. The fighting arrogance of man, even heightened into his projecting his importance into immortality, should perhaps be checked. We have overstepped and perhaps we should seek to be closer to nature because the Kingdom that Jesus speaks about is a funny Kingdom. Its prototypes are the children, the lilies, and the birds. And one of the things that is going on right now as you meditate on the Kingdom and on Jesus is that we start to understand the importance of seeking ourselves closer to the vibrations of nature. I don't know if you have noticed one of the signs of the generation gap, or whatever you want to call it, but one of them is actually that where my generation spoke about "civilized" the kids speak about "humanized"; and that's two very different things, and the Kingdom where the child is the ideal is closer to the "humanized" than to the "civilized".

I think that is one of the reasons there is such an attraction and a sound attraction towards Eastern religions who have not glorified man by immortality, but rather have seen man finding himself by taking a lower and a lower posture even all the way toward Nirvana. And this has made Eastern religious man sensitive and given him, strangely enough, the tremendous respect for life, for other men's lives, because he didn't 'up' his own life with a kind of ferocious and arrogant intensity which we might have done. In times of demonic over-power and super-powers and over-kill, there is wisdom in the low posture of the East.

So, sisters and brothers, we are very small but we are small in the hands of God. Hence we do not need to up our importance. George Wald pointed out with striking clarity that man has his immortality in the germ plasm, but man has always liked to have it in his body. And I would add: for a long period of the Christian tradition, he liked to have it in the soul. But perhaps this whole search for identity perpetuation or immortality as assurance should be lifted out of the ego and be placed in God. To me it seems that if God is God, I neither care for nor worry about the hereafter; I celebrate the coming of the Kingdom by singing hymns and by caressing with words the heaven with angels and saints and the messianic banquet with light and joy and glory. And I know that I paint, but I like to paint and I paint out of love and hope and faith. But when all is said and done I pray that the evil I have put into the world will not cause others to suffer too much, and that my little life will fit somehow into God's plan for the Kingdom. The rest I leave. May His Kingdom come.

Bibliography

For further references and bibliography, see K. Stendahl (ed.), *Immortality and Resurrection* with articles by Oscar Cullmann, Harry A. Wolfson, Werner Jaeger, and Henry J. Cadbury (New York: Macmillan Paperback, 1965).

The Old Testament and Early Jewish texts are interpreted by George Nickelsburg, Jr., *Resurrection, Immortality, and Eternal Life in Intertestamental Judaism* (Cambridge, Mass.: Harvard Theological Studies 26, 1972).

Significant comparative material is available in S.G.F. Brandon, *The Judgment of the Dead: The Idea of Life After Death in the Major Religions* (New York: Charles Scribner's Sons, 1967).

For contemporary theology, see Gordon D. Kaufman, *Systematic Theology* (New York: Charles Scribner's Sons, 1968), pp. 464–474; and H.A. Williams, *True Resurrection* (New York: Holt, Rinehart and Winston, 1972).